FIRESEEDS
OF
SPIRITUAL
AWAKENING

FIRESEEDS OF SPIRITUAL AWAKENING
by Dan Hayes

A Campus Crusade for Christ book
Published by
HERE'S LIFE PUBLISHERS, INC.
P.O. Box 1576
San Bernardino, CA 92402

Library of Congress Catalog Card 83-073130
ISBN 0-86605-130-9
HLP Product No. 403220
© 1983 Campus Crusade for Christ, Inc.

Printed in the United States of America.
Scripture quotations are from the New American Standard
Bible, © The Lockman Foundation 1960, 1962, 1963, 1968, 1971,
1972, 1973, 1975, and are used by permission.

CONTENTS

Preface

Acknowledgments

Notes

Preface

This is an exciting time to be alive on the college campus!

Like an impending earthquake, there is a rumbling under the ground that is beginning to swell to exceptional proportions. The Christian collegians of America are about to experience more joy, power, challenge, and significance than at any time in recent memory.

God is beginning to draw together from all corners of our land a spiritual force of students which will obliterate the massive apathy and purposelessness that has afflicted our nation for some years.

Yes, spiritual awakening is coming to the campuses and coming soon.

This book is written to help you and me get "on board," to get caught in the joyous jetstream of God's Spirit as He sweeps over the "ivy-covered" walls of America.

In these pages can be found the motivation, perspective, methods and results of massive spiritual stirrings in our dorms, fraternities, sororities, athletic teams and classes.

My prayer for myself, and for you, is that we may be stirred, motivated and instructed to see a great spiritual revolution come to the halls of academia. If we expect it and follow the principles outlined here, we'll see it happen. Why not jump in with me and let's see what we can find.

Dan Hayes

Acknowledgments

John Donne said, "No man is an island." Certainly that is true when it comes to writing a book; no man writes by himself. Therefore, I would like to offer my sincere thanks to the following who have helped in the endeavor.

Dr. William R. Bright gave me the encouragement to begin this undertaking.

Judy Steward spent many hours working on the manuscript.

Roger Randall and the Campus Crusade campus team helped me discern the needs of college students and offered many helpful suggestions on the book itself.

Ney Bailey, by her own example as an author and speaker, spurred me on when the going got rough.

Les Stobbe and the staff of Here's Life Publishers gave excellent critique and editing to these efforts.

And, most of all, my wife, Charlotte, and children, Janie and Danny, exhibited the sort of love and patience that was necessary to allow this book to be written.

1

Let's Turn The College Campus Right-side Up

Headline in the *Atlanta Journal,* Feb. 20, 1983:
"80's Students Embrace Cash, Not Causes."

If you have just read the above headline, you are probably one of the 11½ million college students in America today. If so, the odds are better than one in four that you are also a Christian, not only because you are reading a book on spiritual awakening, but also because 26 percent of American college students today claim to be Christians. This percentage is probably the largest in America in the last forty years.

But what that headline says is also true. College students today have ceased to embrace causes and have turned their attention instead to how they can grab for all the material wealth and security they can in this life. The irony of the situation is that even Christian students have bought into this type of philosophy. We, who ought to be the salt of the earth and the light of the world, have instead become the vanilla extract and the bushel baskets.

As I travel on campuses, I look for revolutionary Christians who will stand up and say they're committed to living for Christ, no matter what the cost and no matter what they, seemingly, might have to sacrifice. But it's hard to find such Christians. However, *if* there are nearly 2½ million Christian college students on campus today, as statistics indicate, something needs to change and I believe that you and I can be the agents of that change.

Now don't get me wrong—college is and should be fun. Nowhere else can you make the kind of friends that you'll make in college; nowhere else can you reach new academic horizons like you can in the universities. Nowhere else can you have dates like the ones you'll have in college (maybe). Nowhere else can you be trained for employment like you'll be trained in college. Nowhere else can you get that first feeling of freedom that you get in college. Nowhere else can you have the joy of self discovery that you have in college. I don't think God is a mean old man looking out over the battlements of heaven for someone who is having fun. And, then, as soon as He sees someone having a good time, He leans out, points His finger and says "ah ha, fun, fun! The first three letters of funeral for that person." There is no question that four of the greatest years of my life were in college, and some of you are cramming those four years into five, six, seven or eight, so you should have double the fun.

The Sexual Revolution and the Christian

But let's look more deeply. What is really happening on your campus today? Recently I spoke at Duke University on the subject of "Sex and The Search for Intimacy." My thesis was that the sexual revolution that began in the '60s has been a resounding success and a tragic failure. Part of my presentation was to encourage my audience to save themselves sexually until marriage. The response of the group, the majority of whom did not know Christ, was remarkable. Student after student came up to me and said, "You know, Dan, you're exactly right. After hearing what you had to say tonight, I have decided to stop sleeping around." The sad thing about this was that not only were non-Christians making these comments but also those who were Christians. From these conversations it was apparent that sexual looseness is the norm on campus today.

Goals Without Purpose

Lack of purpose is also rampant. If you ask average students what their purpose in life is, they will say to get a degree and then get a job, buy a house, and have a family. If you ask them what their purpose will be after that, they will most likely say that they will want to get a bigger job, a bigger house, a bigger family and perhaps even a bigger mate. Beyond that, they have no purpose. In fact, most people I meet have goals but no overarching sense of purpose to govern those goals. They bounce from objective to objective, event to event, with no anchor to steady their paths. Students of today are just like everyone

11

else—drifting, hoping to find purpose and meaning by landing the right job, only to discover that landing the right position is simply a springboard to trying to find yet another job.

At a major U. S. university, a fraternity president who made straight A's, was involved in student government, and was one of the most popular students on his campus told me he used to lock himself in his room when the day was over and, by his own testimony, stare at the walls for hours because he had no purpose or direction in life.

Not only are students today lost in a sexual morass and a purposeless environment but on campuses across America they also hear the Christian position mocked and disregarded. Dr. Charles Malik, one of the greatest of all world statesmen, has said, "The two places that Jesus would be least welcome today are in the halls of the Kremlin and in the classrooms of America." Battles have gone to the Supreme Court to determine whether it is even permissible for Christians to meet on campus to pray. Christian professors are intimidated by fellow professors for openly espousing a Christian, biblical, or even moral viewpoint. This has forced many Christian professors into being "closet believers," who hold a personal faith but never talk about it or ever influence their students toward it. At the same time, those who espouse a militantly anti-Christian view are blithely dispensing it to all the students they teach.

Full Out or Fallout?

You may be saying, "But wait, Dan, I'm part of a Christian group on campus. I don't fit into any of those categories." If you're part of a group, that's great. But look around you. Would you describe yourself and the other members of your group as being revolutionary Christians who are "full on and full out" for Jesus Christ? Or would you describe yourself as part of a Christian club? Maybe you attend a Christian college, so that some of the remarks I made earlier don't apply completely to you. But ask yourself this question, "Is there revolutionary Christianity on my campus?" Is there an immense amount of spiritual power being released where I attend college?

In the book of 1 Corinthians, chapter 4, verse 20, there is a verse that has exploded like a bomb in my mental and spiritual life. It says this, "For the kingdom of God does not consist in words but in power." In other words, being a Christian is not talking or writing a good game for Jesus Christ or knowing a great deal about Jesus Christ. The kingdom of God is described in terms of spiritual power. Is there spiritual power in my life to see my prayers answered? Is there spiritual power in my life to introduce others to Christ? Is there spiritual power in my life to resist temptation and overcome evil? Is there spiritual power to move men for God and move God down to men through my prayers? Is there spiritual power to disciple others in a way that is life-changing for them and for me?

The tragic answer on most of our campuses, Christian and secular, is that there is no revolutionary fire, even among Christians. There is no world-changing atmosphere. There is no desire to upset the status quo. Christians more often are noted for what they don't do than for the power expressed in their lives. "I don't drink, smoke or chew and I don't go with those who do." Most Christians are straddling the fence for Jesus Christ with one foot in the world and one foot in the kingdom, an uncomfortable perch that's going nowhere.

Making Him Boring

Christians have done the one thing to Christianity and Christ that even Christ's enemies couldn't do. Christ's enemies scourged Him, mocked Him, beat Him, tried Him falsely, hung Him on a cross, jammed a crown of thorns on His head, stuck a spear in His side, and finally sealed Him in a stone-cold tomb. After His resurrection, His enemies even denied that He had ever existed. But with all this, we Christians have done Christ a worse service. We haven't killed Him, but we have made Him *boring.* Instead of Christianity being perceived as the most exciting thing in the universe, we have portrayed it as lukewarm and dull. Instead of pointing to Christ and saying "Hey, He is the greatest thing since roller skates!" we Christians have become just like everyone else, in pursuit of the American dream, while trying to baptize it with Christian cliches. Consequently, those who don't know Christ can legitimately ask the question, "Why would I want to become a Christian? There doesn't seem to be anything very different about those who are."

A further tragedy is that, while unbelievers remain skeptical about Christianity, Christians aren't happy about this situation either. Believers aren't satisfied being on the fence for Jesus Christ because He has put in their hearts a desire to be totally involved for Him. A Christian life of mediocrity, selfishness and fruitlessness only produces frustration and dissipation.

So here we are, with perhaps as many as 2½ million Christian college students who have a desperate need for power, holiness and New Testament vitality to characterize their lives. If their lives were changed, it would have profound impact on the many who do not know Christ, no doubt bringing hundreds of thousands into the kingdom. We must ask, then, what is the solution? How can we meet this need?

The answer is the subject of this book; revival and awakening on the American college campus. I believe God wants to move across all 3,200 of our campuses in sweeping power. I believe He wants to set the campuses aflame for Christ, to cause the believers to get off the fence and live enthusiastically for Him, and to turn the entire educational system right-side up for the kingdom of God.

Zeal Renewed

You may be thinking, "What is this thing called revival? I've heard about it and it sounds like a pretty religious word. It also sounds pretty boring. What is it, anyway?" Well, the word has been around for nearly four thousand years but in our day it is completely misunderstood. Charles

Finney, the great clergyman of the last century, who was responsible for helping much of America find revival said, "Revival is nothing more than renewed zeal to obey God." That's all, simply renewed desire to be obedient to the God who made us and who always makes plans for our welfare. Obviously, this can happen on a personal level and often does. Individuals are changed and begin to move from selfishness to selflessness, from self-centeredness to love, from anger to patience, and from turmoil to inner peace. But while this happens all the time to individuals, I am going to use the term revival in a different way. Revival also means a moving of God among great masses of people so that multitudes are turned very quickly to renewed zeal to obey God. Many such revivals are mentioned in Scripture and there have been many in church history. The subject of this book is to point out some that have happened on the college campuses of America but, more to the point, to indicate how revival can happen again right now in this collegiate generation.

In every century, starting in the early 1700s moving through the 1800s and into the early 1900s, there has been at least one and in some cases two or three sweeping movements of God's Spirit through the college campuses of America. The results of these movements were that Christians were renewed, sexual looseness changed to holiness, apathy to zeal, impotence to power, hate to love, indifference into passion, and carnality into spirituality. The result among unbelievers was equally startling. In some cases, one-third to one-half of the students of a university were af-

16

fected, giving their hearts and lives publicly to Jesus Christ, and going on to become fruitful disciples for Him. The universities involved in such revivals were not unknown. There were schools like Yale, Harvard, University of North Carolina, Baylor, Emory, Cornell, Northwestern, The University of Illinois and many others, where thousands were converted and discipled and, after graduating, made a tremendous impact upon society for good and for God. For example, at Princeton University:

In 1875, a student Christian group known as the Philadelphia Society had 110 active members. Luther Wishard, who became the group's president in 1876, united the society with the Y.M.C.A. movement (which at that time was committed to evangelism and discipleship....)

The objectives of the Intercollegiate Y.M.C.A. as framed by Wishard included:

1. The importance of seeking the salvation of students for their own sake and their influence as educated men.
2. The importance of securing their salvation while in college.
3. The value of united work and prayer.

"The methods for achieving these objectives included:

1. Diligent study of the Word of God.
2. Prayer.
3. Personal work (one-to-one evangelism).
4. Efficient organization.

Through Wishard's leadership and the student's prayers, evangelist Dwight L. Moody was persuaded to conduct a series of evangelistic meetings on campus. As a result *nearly one third of the student body indicated they received Christ.* Among those working with the Princeton Y.M.C.A. were some of the most outstanding campus leaders. One such student evangelist was Tommy Wilson, who eventually became president of Princeton University. Later still, he became better known as T. Woodrow Wilson, *28th president of the United States.*[2]

Such experiences were common in American colleges and universities. Believers were stirred for God and thereby changed. Unbelievers were so stunned by these movings of God's Spirit and the difference in the lives of Christians, that they came in droves to give their lives to Christ and to become part of great movements on their campuses. Christian society swelled, mission movements advanced, morality on campuses changed, professors were converted and taught from a Christian value system, great American leaders like Woodrow Wilson came out of the movement, and major segments of the life of America as well as the life of the world were affected.

A Forty-Year Wait

The last such massive movement on American campuses occurred nearly eighty years ago in 1905. Virtually every campus in America was touched by that awakening. In fact, perhaps as many as ten to fifteen thousand missionaries went overseas from college campuses because of what God did in that awakening of 1905. Up until that time, such collegiate awakenings occurred approximately every forty years but since 1905—nothing. We are forty years overdue!

Collegiate revival can and, I believe, is going to occur in our day. In fact, you and I may be the spark plugs to help make it happen on the campuses that we influence. Dr. James Stewart, an outstanding minister in Scotland, said, "If we could but show the world that being a follower of Christ is no tame, humdrum, sheltered monotony but the most exciting experience the human spirit can know, then those who are standing outside the church looking askance at Christ would come crowding into our churches to pay Him allegiance and we might well see the greatest revival since Pentecost." We can help make this happen on our campuses.

Joining with hundreds of thousands of students on hundreds of campuses across America, we can have a part in seeing American college campuses change and in influencing the history not only of the university but also of our country for the next one hundred years. Charles Finney said, "One way that we may know that revival is coming is when it is desperately needed."[3] *It is* desperately needed on the college campuses today. That is one reason I believe it is coming and coming soon.

Turning Campuses Right-side Up

This book is designed to help you as a student become a spark plug for spiritual revolution and revival on your campus. You may be only one person but by grabbing hold of the principles in this book, you can be used of God to influence thousands of fellow students for Jesus Christ. You can help turn the campuses of America right-side up for the Savior.

In the next chapter, we will look at a revival instigated by a sixteen-year-old boy that shook an entire population for God. We will also examine an awakening launched by a twenty-six-year-old college student that resulted in one hundred thousand people becoming Christians in the span of three months.

But before we look at that chapter, let me suggest an action point from this chapter. Would you pause and ask God to make you willing to be one of those people who will help spark a revival for God on your campus? You may have great natural abilities and you may not; that isn't the issue. It is not your ability that God is looking for but your availability. So would you, right now, before reading any further, tell the Lord that you desire to be available to Him to be used to help spark revival on your campus? Join with me and thousands of others who want to help shape the campuses of America through revival. Don't be trapped by seeking cash rather than the greatest cause of all, that of Jesus Christ.

2

Revived at Sixteen;

Reviver at Twenty-six

At all ages the great creative religious ideas have been the achievement of the intellectual and spiritual insight of young men. This is evidenced by such names as Jesus, St. Francis of Assissi, Savonarola, Loyola, Huss, Luther, Erasmus, Wesley, and Mott... Many of the most revolutionary ideas have been worked out by young men under 30 and frequently by youths between 18 and 25.

Clarena P. Shedd[1]

For me, this has to be one of the most significant and encouraging quotes that has been given to the college students of today. So often I have heard the question, "Can we as students in the 1980s really do anything significant? We're so young. We don't have any resources. We're just studying to get through school."

However, the fact of the matter is that throughout history, where God has been at work, He has used young men and women to accomplish His

21

tasks, to further His purposes, to interject into history those awakenings that have changed its very course. In fact, without young men and women being available to God, many of the great movements of history would never have occurred.

In this chapter we want to look at an awakening that literally shook a nation and that was started through a 20-year-old. We want to get a picture both from the Word of God and also from more contemporary illustrations not only of what God can do through people who are given to Him, young or not, but also how He can do it. What are the criteria? What are the principles that God uses? What are the benefits? If we can grab hold of these principles, and understand them, then I believe we can literally shake our campuses for God in a way that much of the agnosticism and religious and Christian apathy that now exists there will be changed into heart-felt searching and finding of God and of His Son, Jesus Christ.

The Worst of Times

The awakening we want to look at takes place in the Old Testament in 2 Chronicles 33 and 34. Described here are the worst of times and the best of times. All that is left of Israel is the southern kingdom of Judah, the northern ten tribes having been taken into captivity some years before. Judah was ruled by a succession of evil and good kings. In Chapter 33, we see two of the worst of the worst, Manasseh and Amon.

Manasseh, who ruled for fifty-five years, had the distinction of being one of the worst kings who ever ruled any nation in the history of the world.

In fact, he was so bad that God said about him, "Thus Manasseh misled Judah and the inhabitants of Jerusalem to do more evil than the nations whom the Lord destroyed before the sons of Israel" (verse 9). In other words, he was even worse than the heathen kings of the heathen nations around him. To make matters worse, he ruled for an incredibly long time. It was like having Adolf Hitler rule for fifty-five years.

Not content with his own evil, Manasseh spent most of his time involving everyone else in his sin. Second Chronicles 33:2 tells us that "he did evil in the sight of the Lord according to the *abominations* of the nations whom the Lord dispossessed before the sons of Israel." In verse 17 it is said that his influence was so great that the people still sacrificed to idols.

When Manasseh died, his son Amon took over. He was much like his father, but not quite as creative. Second Chronicles 33:22 says, "He did evil in the sight of the Lord as Manasseh his father had done, and Amon sacrificed to all the carved images which his father Manasseh had made, and he served them." Some of the brighter things that Amon and Manasseh did in Israel were to practice witchcraft and spiritism (2 Chronicles 33:6). But they also encouraged people to sacrifice their children to the gods of Molech and Baal. In some cases, this means that babies were sacrificed on altars of fire. About the only good thing you can say about Amon is that he only ruled two years; he was so obnoxious that his own servants finally conspired against him and put him to death in his own house.

Josiah, the Child-King

Let's face it: Judah was in a bad way. They had just had fifty-seven years under Manasseh and Amon filled with idolatry, witchcraft, murder, immorality and all manner of heathen practices. The people had forgotten about the living God. They were materialistic. They wanted their own way and they were uninterested in any sort of spiritual awakening. But it has been well said that the darker the night, the brighter the light. And into this dark situation strides the protagonist in the *good news* part of this drama, Josiah the king. Second Chronicles 34:1-3 tells us: "Josiah was eight years old when he became king, and he reigned thirty one years in Jerusalem. And he did right in the sight of the LORD, and he walked in the ways of his father David and did not turn aside to the right or to the left. For in the eighth year of his reign while he was still a youth, he began to seek the God of his father David and in the twelfth year he began to purge Judah and Jerusalem of the high places, the Asherim, the carved images, and the molten images."

Josiah, the Praying Teenager

What a contrast to his grandfather and to his father, proving again that like father, like son is not always true. In three verses the scene has completely changed. Only eight years old when he started to reign, Josiah evidently had within him a heart for God from the earliest age. At age sixteen he began to seek God fervently and earnestly. No doubt this yearning and prayer changed his entire life and reign into one that was

24

given over to seeking the glory of God and to making Jerusalem and Judah the righteous kingdom that God had always intended it to be. How it must have grieved his righteous heart to see the practices of the palace around him and those of the nation that was named with God's own name. How many hours he must have prayed and wept, and thought and planned and strategized and studied until, gradually, ideas and directions came into focus that he knew were what he had to do, though he was still a young man by any standard.

The Scripture says that at the age of twenty (the twelfth year of his reign) he began to purge Judah and Jerusalem of the high places, the Asherim, the carved images, and the molten images. What you have to appreciate about Josiah at this point is that he never hid behind his youth to excuse inaction. He never used as an excuse his potential powerlessness. He never said, "Well, I know things are really bad and what this society is doing certainly isn't glorifying God, but after all, what can I do? Sure, I'm king, but I have all these advisors around me and they're so much older and they constantly caution me not to take any steps that would upset the applecart or cause political upheaval in my kingdom or stop people from paying taxes or have them request a recall election to find a new king. I just don't think I'd better do anything very radical now while I'm so young. I'll just wait until I become fifty or sixty years of age; then I'll be so respected that people will listen to me and I can make all the changes I need to make."

I think Josiah had a totally different view of his own youth. I believe he realized that he was in a prime position at that age to accomplish the total renewal and revival of his nation and society. He knew he had the energy. He knew he was not tied down by as many responsibilities as he would be when he was older. He knew that, as a young man, he was still idealistic. He knew that, though he still had much to learn, he also had a lot of time to learn it. And I believe he knew that he could count on other men and women of his own age and convictions to follow him and form an army that would help accomplish the cleansing of what remained of Israel.

Josiah ranged far afield from Jerusalem. In verses 6 and 7 of chapter 34 we read that in the cities of Manasseh, Ephraim, and Simeon, even as far as Naphtali, and their surrounding ruins, he also tore down the altars and beat the Asherim and carved images into powder and chopped down all incense altars throughout the land of Israel. Then he returned to Jerusalem. To me this is a great story. Can you imagine this young man, no doubt the leader of a force of other young men and women (verse 4) all over the country, whose desire was to destroy the very things that had brought dishonor to God. Josiah and his followers encouraged the people to return to God, confronting all the religious apathy, all the entrenched idolatry, and all the wickedness arrayed against him. In the face of opposition he burned white hot with a passion for God and righteousness. This passion not only drove him, but caused the engaging of many others to follow him. And evidently, in the space of about six short years, all of Israel was, at least, outwardly cleansed of the idolatrous practices that had characterized the two previous kings. Can you imagine? He turned the whole nation around in six short years. That's how long it takes some people just to get through college.

But even though Israel was outwardly cleansed of its unrighteousness, the deeper problem of inward cleansing and inward renewal remained. The truth is that, while you can legislate law, you cannot legislate spirituality. That can only come from inside an individual and from inside a population. Josiah had made the right start and had indeed accomplished more in a few short years than most people could accomplish in an entire lifetime. But how could the inward transformation of Israel be accomplished?

Josiah, the Righteous Young Man

At age twenty-six, while Josiah was no doubt pondering both the successes of his reign and what remained to be accomplished, a discovery was made during the cleaning and restoration of the temple. Second Chronicles 34:14 tells us that Hilkiah the priest found a lost book of the Law of the Lord given by Moses. Evidently this book had been lost at least since the beginning of Manasseh's reign, some eighty years. Most scholars believe that this volume was the book of Deuteronomy, the restatement of the Law, the reminder to the people of Israel not to forsake their God, and the warnings to them of what would happen if in fact they did forsake Him. The implication in Chapter 34 is that Josiah had never seen this book. But as he began to study and read it, its effect upon him was profound and devastating.

Second Chronicles 34:19 tells us, "And it came about when the king heard the words of the law that he tore his clothes." Throughout Scripture whenever people tear their clothes it is always a mark of great sorrow and grief, and repentance. It seems always to be felt when there is a renewed consciousness of the holiness, the majesty, and the presence of God Himself. It must have dawned upon Josiah that for eighty years no one had read this book; no one had believed it; no one had followed it; everybody had simply forgotten it.

No wonder, Josiah must have thought, *we have experienced such immorality and unrighteousness in our kingdom. No wonder the people are so spiritually bankrupt. We have not only not obeyed God, we have not even known what obeying God means.*

As we've seen, Josiah was not the kind of person to simply sit and ponder what he wanted to do. He immediately took action. Verses 29-33 of 2 Chronicles 34 tells us not only what action Josiah took, but the long-term response of the people to Josiah's life and to their exposure, through him, to the Word of God.

"Then the king sent and gathered all the elders of Judah and Jerusalem. And the king went up to the house of the Lord and all the men of Judah, the inhabitants of Jerusalem, the priest, the Levites, and all the people, from the greatest to the least; and he read in their hearing all the words of the book of the covenant which was found in the house of the Lord. Then the king stood in his place and made a covenant before the LORD, to walk after the LORD, and to keep His commandments and His testimonies and His statutes, with all his heart and with all his soul, to perform the words of the covenant written in this book. Moreover, he made all who were present in Jerusalem and Benjamin to stand *with him*. So the inhabitants of Jerusalem did according to the covenant of God, the God of their fathers. And Josiah removed all the abominations from all the lands belonging to the sons of Israel, and made all who were present in Israel to serve the LORD their God. Throughout his lifetime they did not turn from following the LORD God of their fathers."

God had undertaken to solve the second part of Josiah's dilemma, namely, how to produce the inward change that would connect with the outward cleansing that Josiah had accomplished in all Judah. And He had done this by providing the power of His own Word, which not only cut like a sword through Josiah and his friends, but also through the people at large.

Revival of a Lifetime

If you will notice the last part of the passage quoted above, throughout Josiah's entire lifetime the people did not turn from following the Lord God of their fathers. No longer did they simply follow Josiah, nor did they exhibit simply a rigorous, fearful adherence to his kingly position. The people now, in their hearts, came under the conviction of God's Word and desired to serve Him from within. The next chapter of 2 Chronicles tells us that once again the Passover was celebrated as it had not been celebrated in centuries. In fact, this was probably the greatest Passover in all of Israel's history, ever since its inception on that dark night in Egypt. This was not a legalistic response to Josiah, but a heartfelt enthusiasm and refreshing that the entire nation experienced on both an individual and a corporate level. Awakening had come!

Don't you think it incredible what God did through this very young leader, who was only twenty six years of age by the time all this had been accomplished? Doesn't that give you encouragement concerning what God can do through you and me, even in our youth? Isn't it exciting to think about seeing an entire nation turn around, or an entire campus or dormitory, or fraternity or sorority, or athletic team? If it could happen through Josiah, it can happen through you and me.

But wait, you say, Josiah was a king, and I'm a nobody. Kings can always get their wills accomplished but I can't even get my roommate to pick up his socks. There had been plenty of other kings before Josiah, even good ones, who hadn't influenced the people the way he did. What was it that was different about Josiah and what can be different about us on our campuses today? I believe there are four basic principles that allowed Josiah to be the influence that he was to help accomplish the revival that occurred.

Only God

First Josiah was effective because he knew that being king alone would make no difference, that it was only God who could produce a spiritual awakening in that apostate nation. He *knew he had to pray.* When the Scripture says that Josiah "began to see God at age sixteen," a great part of that was prayer.

It has always been this way; the people who move and shake our world are not necessarily the ones who appear in the newspapers but the people who pray.

Yes, you say, but can that really happen today? Let me tell you the story of Samuel J. Mills of Williams College. In April of 1806, "as an entering freshman at Williams College Samuel Mills cut anything but an impressive figure. Mills was described by one of his roommates as having 'an awkward figure and ungainly manner and an inelastic and croaking voice.' But the situation was even more discouraging, for although no one could have known it at the time, scarcely a dozen years remained to Mills' life. In this context his achievements are remarkable.

"Soon after his arrival he came into contact with a group of fellow Christians who were meeting in prayer for revival among students of Williams College. Fearful of contempt and possible disruption from their peers, the group met in the countryside some distance from the college. Although he was but a freshman he was also twenty-three and because of his maturity and the depth and sincerity of his own religious life, Mills quickly became the leader of these students.

The Haystack Prayer Meeting

"The group continued to meet on a twice weekly basis throughout the summer. One hot, sultry August afternoon, the skies began to darken and the accompanied thundershowers and lightning persuaded them to return to the shelter of the college buildings. Before they could reach the campus, however, the clouds began to disperse and they were able to continue their meeting under the shelter of a nearby haystack. After some discussion, Mills invited the students to join with him in offering their lives in the cause of foreign missions, so as to reach the under-privileged peoples of the world. 'We can do this if we will,' he said, revealing a determination differing from the expected 'we will do this if we can'."[2]

This haystack prayer meeting was the beginning of a great awakening at Williams College and the beginning of the modern foreign missions movement from within the United States. The impact of the revival was so great that, as J. Edwin Orr tells us, "not only Williams College, but also Yale, Amherst, Dartmouth, Princeton, to name a few, reported the conversion to God of a *third to a half of their total student bodies*, which in those days usually numbered between 100-250."[3]

As with Josiah, it was the prayers of Samuel Mills and his compatriots that not only sparked a great awakening in Williams College, and indeed in all of New England, but also launched one of the greatest foreign missions thrusts in the history of the world. All because they were willing to pray.

Josiah, the Activist

Second, I believe Josiah was effective, even as a young man, in the awakening of his day, because he took action concerning his convictions. In 2 Chronicles 34:3, it not only says that he began to *seek* the God of his father David, but that in the twelfth year of his reign he began to *purge* Judah and Jerusalem of the high places, the carved images, and the molten images. Josiah was an activist. He knew that he could not do everything, but he knew that he could do something. He also knew that by his example and leadership others might be motivated to be activists in their spheres of influence. No doubt it was quite lonely being out on the cutting edge, but as he began to watch others fall into step with him, and perhaps in some cases, accomplish more than he, it made all the loneliness and hardship worth it.

Taking a stand and being an activist is not an easy thing to do, particularly when you may receive ridicule from students, professors, townspeople, and others. But it always seems to pay.

I remember a friend of mine in college, a fellow student named Bruce. He and I had been Christians about the same length of time, about one year. We both had a professor of English who was renowned among the faculty as a skeptic. His classes numbered three or four hundred every semester and he delighted in taking every opportunity he could to discredit the Bible and the gospel of Jesus Christ. Semester after semester unknowing students, including myself, would write down what he said as truth and find their faith, if they had any at all in the Word of God and Christianity, completely undermined. He was a very intimidating man and would make a point of ridiculing anyone who would stand for his faith.

Consequently my approach was, "I'm just going to keep quiet and try and suffer through this semester and hope I don't get ridiculed."

Bruce the Activist

But my friend Bruce took a different tack. He decided he was going to become an activist and not allow his beliefs to be trampled without a struggle. One afternoon he approached this professor and, trembling, challenged him on a statement he had made concerning two sets of ten commandments in the Old Testament, each of which contradicted the other. The professor, somewhat grudgingly, pulled out a Bible from his shelf, blew the dust off it, and opened it to show my friend the error of his way. After a pause of a few minutes, while the professor searched for the two allegedly conflicting passages, he looked up with a surprised expression. To Bruce's amazement he said, "Well, what do you know. There are two sets of ten commandments in Scripture, *but they don't contradict each other after all.*"

As far as I know, that professor never taught that falsehood again. All because Bruce was willing to stand up for his faith and be willing to be an activist, even when his grades might have been at stake. This experience emboldened him to become a more aggressive witness for Christ.

As you study history, you become convinced that the people who changed the world have not necessarily been the smartest, nor the richest, nor the most powerful in terms of political structures; they have been people who have been willing to be activists for their faith, even when their faith has been misplaced. I am not counseling irresponsible activism, but an activism based upon God's Word. Such activism effectively "chooses its place to take its stand" where it will move the maximum number of people toward seeing that Jesus Christ is the King of kings and Lord of lords.

Honest About Sin

Not only was Josiah a man of prayer, and an activist, but he was *also honest about his own sins and the sins of his people.* In 2 Chronicles 34:19 and 21, we read that not only did Josiah personally repent and tear his clothes when he realized his sin of ignoring the law, but he was aware that by the peoples' trampling the law of God there was a dire expectation of judgment upon them. His response in verse 27 was to confess his sin and the sins of his people and then to expose his people to the Word of God that they might personally repent and confess, and cleansing might occur. This cleansing affected not only individuals but the nation.

A New Testament passage focusing on cleansing says, "If we confess our sins, He is faithful and righteous to forgive us our sins and to cleanse us from all unrighteousness" (1 John 1:9). Notice that confession means to agree with God that our sins are wrong, forgiven, and to be turned from.

Josiah did not try to hide his sin, though as king he perhaps had more justification for doing so than anyone else. He didn't try to blame others for his sins or belittle them. He acknowledged them and asked the Lord to cleanse him. That is what we must do if we are to experience God's power in our lives and be avenues of God for spiritual awakening and revival.

The Student Preacher

Less than eighty years ago, there was another young man who was not afraid to call his compatriots to confession and repentance. He was Evan Roberts, age 26, of Wales. Roberts, a student at Newcastle Emlyn College, had had a profound experience with God in which he experienced cleansing and awakening in his own life. With the permission of his college principal, Roberts left his studies and went home to the village of Loughor to preach his first sermon. Only seventeen people waited to hear his first message, but he gave them four points: to confess any known sin to God and to put right any wrong done to man, to put away any doubtful habit, to obey the Holy Spirit promptly, and to confess faith in Christ openly. No one could have imagined the response.

Dr. J. Edwin Orr tells us that "within three months a hundred thousand converts had been added to the churches of Wales. Five years later a book debunking the revival was published and the main point made by the scholarly author was that of the 100,000 added to the churches, only 80,000 remained after five years."

Roberts was not afraid to call sin by its name, not in a self-righteous sense, but in a sense of asking for cleansing and forgiveness, and then encouraging others to do the same. The Spirit of God took the simple words of this godly young man and not only turned a whole nation right-side up for righteousness, but used his words to begin a spiritual awakening that circled the globe within the next five years. It is estimated that millions came to Christ worldwide.

Josiah, the Caller of People

There's a fourth and final example of Josiah that we, no matter how old or young, may follow to be used of God to turn our campuses and communities back to Him. *That is, Josiah was not afraid to call other people to come alongside him and pursue the same ends.* We read in 2 Chronicles 34:30, "that the king went up to the house of the LORD, and all the men of Judah, the inhabitants of Jerusalem, the priests, the Levites, and all the people, from the greatest to the least; and he read in their hearing all the words of the book of the covenant which was found in the house of the LORD."

Josiah was not simply reading the people a bedtime story for his idle pleasure or just giving them information. He was reading to them so that they might hear and yield their lives and obey the God of heaven and earth. He was calling them to become, if you will, a part of a great army for righteousness in that day, an army that would be an army of love and of holiness and of support to those who wanted to live for God. He knew he could not do alone the work he had been given; it was necessary that tens, hundreds, and thousands of others be involved in the same great task of walking with the Lord and of being a witness to the nations around him.

We can do that; in fact, we have to do that.

None of us is strong enough, spiritual enough, talented enough, or smart enough on our own to be the only channel of blessing for our campuses or our communities. However, each of us can call other people to be on our team. And as other people join with us, they can call still others to be a part. By a few each calling a few, who call a few more, very quickly a great movement can be built. Such a movement not only will permeate every segment of our campuses, but will also become a channel of spiritual power which will, in the providence of the Holy Spirit, touch the inner lives of students in ways we could never touch them by our words, our persuasiveness, or our personalities.

David Bryant, missions specialist for Inter-Varsity Christian Fellowship, reports on an awakening at Wheaton College in 1980-81. He tells us of five students—not ten, not one hundred, but five students—who began to pray for the mobilization of believers on that campus in prayer for the world. The implication in his report is not only did they pray, but they also called other students to that same sort of prayer. By the end of that school year there were no longer simply five students praying for world evangelization. There were sixty dormitory prayer groups praying for the evangelization of the world. Think of it. From five students to over three hundred in one year, simply because those few students decided to pray and call other students to be involved in this same task of helping to reach the world.

Here's the point—spiritual awakening frequently starts with young men and women willing to go out on a limb for Jesus Christ, to pray fervently for spiritual awakening, to live out and be activists for the biblical convictions they have, to be honest in confessing their own sins and the sins of the campus or community in which they live, and to be unafraid to expose others to that same Word and Spirit from which conviction comes. And, finally, spiritual awakening comes from those who are willing to call others to the same challenge and the task with which they themselves have been burdened.

Think back on Evan Roberts. He was only twenty-six; his first sermon was heard by only seventeen people; he had not finished his college degree; and he was not an accomplished preacher. Yet he was willing to pray, to be an activist, to call others to come with him and be honest about their sins; God used him and the others he reached to see one hundred thousand people added to the kingdom of Christ.

Paul said to Timothy, "Let no one look down on your youthfulness" (1 Timothy 4:12a). As students, we can see God use us, perhaps not in as great a magnitude as Evan Roberts but, again, perhaps in an even greater magnitude. That is up to God. But let us never hide behind our own youth or inexperience to sell ourselves short. The time for spiritual awakening is now and we can be the ones who will ignite it.

Tell the Lord today that you want to be like Josiah. You may be young, but, as I see it, that is an advantage. Ask God to use you to stir up your campus for God, and then watch what He does.

3

The Five Prerequisites to Revival

> Many of you have already found out, and others
> will find out in the course of their lives, that truth
> eludes us if we do not concentrate with total at-
> tention on its pursuit.
>
> Alexander Solzhenitsyn[1]

As we consider revival and awakening on our
campuses, the question we must ask is, "What
is my part in seeing revival and awakening come,
and what is God's part?" In seeking an answer,
there are two things to keep in mind. First, God
Himself is the only source of revival. He brings
it, He establishes it, He conserves it. The second
thing to remember is that God often waits in
bringing revival until we have exercised our own
faith and obedience. Thus there are two parts: our
part and His part. We cannot do His part, but
we *can* do our part. Dr. G. Campbell Morgan once
said: "We cannot organize revival, but we can set
our sails to catch the wind from heaven when God
chooses to blow upon His people once again."[2]

As we study revivals in God's Word and from
more recent history, there seem to be five prere-

quisites that "set our sails" toward revival. I believe we can express this pattern on our campuses today. If we do that, then perhaps God will be pleased to bring spiritual explosions to the campuses of our country and those around the world. In the next few chapters, we shall look at each prerequisite for awakening and revival. We shall also seek to show one or more examples in history of how each was carried out, along with the resulting effects.

The five prerequisites God's people must meet are:

1. Recognize the need for revival.
2. Humble themselves before God.
3. Confess their sins and repent.
4. Begin to pray continuously for revival.
5. Call other people to join them in praying.

In this chapter we will look in depth at the first prerequisite.

God's People must Recognize the Need for Revival

If you polled a thousand Christian students on campus today regarding the moral apathy, spiritual breakdown, lack of purpose, and struggle with sin that exists on our campuses, and then asked, "Do you think we need a revival today?" no doubt most of them would answer, "Yes, of course we need a revival on our campus." But that is not the kind of need recognition that I am talking about here.

Admitting something and being absolutely gripped to do anything about it are two different things. As Crawford Loritts has said, " 'Is-ness' and 'ought-ness' are two very different things." My son might agree that he needs a bath after a busy day spent covering himself with all the flora and fauna that exist on planet Earth; but though he recognizes that he *needs* a bath, he will *never* take one on his own. He needs a great deal of encouragement.

By recognizing the need for revival, I mean that at least a few Christians on campus are gripped enough with the urgency of the current need to shake their college or university. They want "to paint the house or get off the ladder." They are not content to wring their hands in pious concern. They want to become personally involved in doing something to help bring revival to their campus.

For example: I recently received a letter from a student at Marshall University in West Virginia. In it, he described the concern that a group of students on his campus had for seeing spiritual awakening occur. Their commitment is shown in this portion of his letter: "Big things are happening at Marshall University in Huntington, West Virginia! *Each day* of our spring semester students involved met for prayer at 7 a.m. ....."

Now you and I both know the difficulty of getting most students up at 7 a.m. for anything, even a class. Therefore I would have to say that these students have definitely been gripped by the need for spiritual awakening on their campus. And, having been gripped, they are taking action to help bring this to pass.

No revival ever comes unless at least a few Christians become inflamed with the need to see such an awakening. Josiah, Evan Roberts, and Samuel Mills were all overwhelmed with the need for change and turn-around in their situations. This is the first step, the first prerequisite, to revival. If a person really sees the need, then he or she will be motivated to do something about it. Those who say they see the need, yet never do anything about it, are only indicating, as surely as if neon signs were flashing from their foreheads, that they are not gripped with its urgency.

In John, chapter two, verses 13 to 22, we find the story of Jesus' cleansing of the temple. You remember that seeing those who were selling oxen, sheep and doves, and those who were changing money in the temple, Jesus made a scourge of cords, drove the moneychangers out of the temple, poured out their money, overturned their tables, and then said, "Take these things away; stop making my Father's house a house of merchandise." Jesus saw a need, to stop the defamation of the temple. He did not do as we often do. He did not wring His hands and say, "Oh, this is a terrible situation. What a mess we have here in this temple. Someone should clean it up. But that's not my job, I'm too busy doing other good things like miracles. And after all, I certainly wouldn't want to offend anyone by being too strong in my point of view."

Jesus not only saw the need, he also did something about it. The editorial comment that John the gospel writer makes after this event sums it up: "His disciples remembered that it was written,

'Zeal for Thy house will consume me' " (John 2:17). The King James version says "Zeal for thine house hath eaten me up." Jesus was "eaten up" with the need to do something about the problem. What consumes you? What consumes me? What consumes the Christians on my campus? What *grips* us? The tragedy is that most of us are gripped or consumed with very little other than our own comfort, preservation and well-being.

Have you yet seen that the need on your campus is so great that you are literally consumed with the desire to see change take place? Have you and your Christian friends yet felt the burden for awakening in such a way that you will take action? Is there anything that grips you so strongly that if God doesn't do it, you will become physically sick? I believe that sort of zeal and fervency, which the Lord himself can and must produce over time, is needed for us to be willing to pay whatever price is necessary to make ourselves available to do our part in bringing revival and awakening to our campus.

I was touched recently by the story of a friend who was clearly gripped by the need of America's college students. His name was Read Williamson, a Methodist minister. He had gone to college with my wife, and had pastored a few years after graduating from seminary.

After his wife gave birth to their second child, Read was diagnosed to have an enlarging brain tumor. Though surgery was performed and medication given, the tumor continued to increase. Eventually Read was hospitalized, having only the use of speech and his left hand. For awhile, he was very discouraged, no longer being able to minister. But he realized that there was at least one thing he *could* do: He could pray. My wife Charlotte visited him in the hospital and spoke with him about the need for awakening and spiritual revival on campus. She gave him a poster referring to the subject, which he placed on the wall opposite his bed so that he could see it. As he viewed that poster, he realized that he had plenty of time to pray for the campuses of America. During his hospitalization, he would often pray and speak with visitors about the need for spiritual awakening and for a great movement of God on the college campuses of America.

Shortly before his death, he slipped into a coma. Ah, his usefulness was over, you say. No! Usually, he would mumble, although his speech usually would be incoherent. But his wife Sandy told me a moving story. She said that sometimes his speech would become more lucid and one could recognize the words he was speaking. Sometimes they were about the family. Frequently, the other words she could recognize were actually prayers for college students and the college campus, that spiritual revival and awakening would come.

Imagine, here was a man of God, at death's door, in a coma, ready to make the great transition from the land of the dying to the land of the living. And that which was on his mind and heart, that which gripped him, even in unconsciousness, was his family and the college campuses of America.

After communicating Read's story to a group of students, I received a letter from a student leader at Virginia Tech. In it he said, "We very much enjoyed your story about Read; I have yet to read it to myself or in a group without crying. Wouldn't it be great if we could all have that kind of commitment to prayer and spiritual revival?"

Yes, wouldn't it?

Probably neither you nor I are currently at death's door. Most of us probably have many years ahead of us to serve Christ on this planet. But if only we could be like Read and be gripped with the need, God might be pleased to send awakening.

In the next chapter we will look at the second prerequisite for revival and awakening: humility. But before we turn to that chapter, let me suggest an action point. Take a piece of paper and list on it at least fifteen reasons why you believe your campus needs spiritual awakening and revival. Keep it in a place where you can see and read it daily.

Make it your daily prayer that God would burden you and your friends with the need for spiritual awakening on your campus.

Talk to one another about the need and hold each other accountable. If you do this, you will find yourself accomplishing much more for our Savior.

4

Humility and Its Role in Revival

> Let it be repeated, there are two views of one's
> life. One is that a man's life is his own, to do with
> as he pleases; the other is that it belongs to
> another and . . . that the other to whom it belongs
> is Christ Himself.
>
> John R. Mott[1]

Mary Graham, an associate of mine, was once going through a very difficult series of circumstances that seemed to have no end. A friend, seeking to comfort her, said, "Mary, I bet all these experiences are making you really humble."

She replied, "Oh no, I couldn't be humble. If I were really humble, I would be so proud of it!"

One man said he would write a book and title it *Perfect Humility and How I Attained It.* Humility inspires a lot of humor, probably because most of us don't know what it is. If we do know, we realize we don't have much of it. Yet from my studies of revivals and awakenings, and from what the Word of God has to say about revival, it is very clear that without humility there can be no revival. Thus, the second prerequisite for revival and spiritual awakening on our campuses is that *God's people must humble themselves before Him.*

At the outset, it might be helpful to clear up two misconceptions. Humility is not thinking less of myself than I ought to think. Sometimes Christians think that humility is saying "I'm a worm, I'm only a worm, I cannot do anything, I will be a doormat to every person, place and thing that wants to walk over me." No! Humility means valuing myself with the same value that God places upon me, namely that Christ was willing to die for me. The dignity of man is defined by the cross of Calvary. And if Jesus Christ was willing to die for me, then I cannot think that I am incapable of doing anything significant for him.

Dr. Howard Hendricks, professor at Dallas Theological Seminary, tells the story of the student who came to him and said, "Professor, pray that I might be nothing."

Dr. Hendricks replied, "No, I won't pray that you'll be nothing. You take that by faith. What I will pray for is that you will believe God to use you because of how significant a person you are due to Christ's death on the cross."

The second misconception is that humility is something some people have and some people don't, and that's just the way it is. Let me clue you in, nobody has humility naturally. Oh, I know some people seem more humble. Some people seem more honest, too, but that doesn't necessarily mean that they are. The fact of the matter is that humility is a quality imparted by God, and it is possible for all men, women and children who know Jesus Christ to see that quality become more and more a part of their lives.

One does not become humble by thinking a great deal about humility. Rather, humility manifests itself in individuals' lives as they focus on something or someone else. Rather than concentrating on the quality they are trying to develop, they forget about themselves in the concentration upon the other person or thing.

Seeing Ourselves in Him

Thus, humility in our context means being occupied with God and seeing ourselves in relationship with Him. It means that we see ourselves as creatures, but we see Him as Creator. We see ourselves as unworthy before Him, but in His eyes as worthy because of Christ's death upon the cross. We see ourselves alone as weak, but we see ourselves in Him as strong. We see ourselves as unable, but we see ourselves in Him as able.

In the context of revival and spiritual awakening, this means that, having seen the need for spiritual awakening (as we discussed in the last chapter), we now bow before the Lord, both personally and corporately, and admit that we cannot produce spiritual awakening, but that He *can* produce it. We admit that if anything is going to change He is the one who is going to change it. We admit that in ourselves we cannot ignite the fire of spiritual revival, but as we ally ourselves with Him, He can ignite a great spiritual bonfire that will spread all over our campus and the campuses of our nation and, potentially, over all the world.

Humility means that we admit we are willing to have fellowship with, pray with, and work with other believers who might think a little differently from us. It means that, although all of our doctrines might not be in the same slots, we are willing to focus on the same ends, namely, that of seeing our campus ablaze for God. Humility means that we are willing to do anything, go anywhere, say anything and, in obedience to Christ, to seize spiritual awakening. In every age and time it has been this sort of humility among believers that has ignited them and allowed them to become channels of the Holy Spirit to draw thousands of Christians and non-Christians to the foot of the cross and then into the world to exalt the name of Christ.

. The place of bowing and prostrating ourselves before the Lord in humility, as it relates to revival, shows itself beautifully in the book of Isaiah, chapter 57, verse 15.

> "For thus says the High and Exalted One, who lives forever, whose Name is Holy, I dwell on a high and holy place, and also with the contrite and lowly of spirit in order to *revive* the spirit of the lowly and to *revive* the heart of the contrite."[5]

Note here that the Lord says that He dwells in two places, first He dwells in a high and holy place; that is, He is lofty, He is exalted. We are as dust before Him. He is Creator and we are creature. We bow before Him because He alone is worthy of our trust and homage.

The Muslims have a saying in Arabic, "*Allahu Akbar*" —"God is great!" This may be only a slogan or war-cry in some cases, yet it communicates how we must see God if we are to be humble before Him. We must view Him as majestic, as awesome, as great. And, in fact, He does dwell in a high, majestic, awesome place, in a sense separated from us by His majesty.

But the great news is that God also dwells somewhere else, in a very different location. According to the above passage He also dwells with the contrite (humble) and lowly of heart. He governs us not only in the lofty distance, great and powerful, but He also lives next to, with, and in those who are humble of heart. He dwells with those who admit their need and bow before Him consciously and meaningfully.

Thus, the moment we as Christian students, faculty or lay people recognize Him as high, lofty and holy, and act accordingly by acknowledging our own creaturely status, weakness and need, He moves His dwelling place onto our level, to be right next to, in and with us, closer than any relative or friend. All of His mighty presence and power becomes our possession, when we yield ourselves to be possessed by Him. He becomes our friend, our power, our strength, the resource to meet every need we have on planet Earth, in our families and on our campuses. The one whose heart burns for revival more than any other now becomes our daily resource to produce revival and awakening among our friends, in our living units, and in our classrooms.

Note in this passage His promise of revival to such people who humble themselves, "... to *revive* the spirit of the lowly, and to *revive* the heart of the contrite."

It is plain that humility is a prerequisite for revival. God here says that He revives humble people, that the very objective of His moving His dwelling place from lofty Heaven to lowly "State U." is to revive the hearts of the believers and awaken those of the unbelievers.

Here is a sobering corollary: God never revives proud people. If we as Christians on our campus say, "We've got it together, and with a little more hard work and money we'll do the job. We don't for revival. Frankly, we could stay on our knees until they fuse to the floor and we'd never see revival, because we're not humble. He only brings revival to those of us who say, "Lord, we can't; but You can." And, as the second prerequisite for awakening, we dare not miss it. We must individually and then corporately, with whatever small group we share and see the same burden and need for spiritual awakening, bow before the Lord and ask him to move His dwelling place from the high and lofty to us, the lowly and contrite.

Billy Graham, A Modern-Day Example

Nowhere has an example of the power and promise of humility become more evident than in the thrilling life of evangelist and Christian statesman Billy Graham. Here is a man who has spoken and preached to more people than any man who has lived since the beginning of the world. During more than forty years of personal ministry, he has maintained godliness, holiness and Christian standards of integrity even in the face of attacks from and defections by others. He has had opportunities for many honors and lucrative financial rewards. Yet he has stayed on track to follow the calling that God gave him, namely to win men and women to Jesus Christ around the world, until the Lord Himself returns. Regarding the nature of humility in his own life and its results, one example is very instructive.

By the middle of 1945, Billy Graham was nearly thirty years old, having already become a moderately well-known evangelist and, in addition, a college president. He divided his responsibilities between his administrative duties at Northwestern College in Minneapolis, Minnesota, and various church and local evangelistic crusades. He had, however, no national recognition, nor did he seem destined for any.

During this period of time, a friend of his, Charles Templeton, also an outstanding young man engaged in evangelism, began to have serious doubts concerning the authenticity and reliability of the Scriptures. Charles went to graduate school to attempt to resolve his doubts, but there they only grew more intense. He and Graham often discussed these concerns, and soon Charles subtly began to challenge Billy's commitment to the authority of Scripture and to suggest that Billy should rethink his position on the Bible. As Charles' doubts grew stronger, so did Billy's struggles. He even developed a terrific pain at the base of his skull, brought about, he said later, by nervous tension and exhaustion. In July and August of 1945, though busy with many speaking engagements, Billy decided to give a great deal of time to prayer and humbling himself before the Lord. The intensity of his struggle was very great. One acquaintance remarked that during an evening prayer meeting at a Christian camp, he overheard Billy throw himself full-length on the dewy grass and pray passionately, "Lord, trust me to do something for You before You come." He further remarked, "Oh, if somehow the Lord could use me a little bit."

Finally, the crisis moment came at Forest Home, a conference center in Southern California. After hearing a secondhand remark that his friend Charles allegedly had made (which implied that if Billy continued to believe, trust and preach the authority of the Bible, his ministry would be curtailed and he would never do anything for God), Billy became deeply disturbed and hurt. John Pollack, in his biography of Billy Graham, describes this time of critical, mental, spiritual and emotional prostrating of himself for the Lord as follows:

> "After supper, instead of attending the evening service, he retired to his log cabin and read again the Bible passage concerning its authority. He recalled someone saying that the prophets used such phrases as 'the Word of God came to us' or 'Thus saith the Lord' more than 2,000 times. He meditated on the attitude of Christ, who fulfilled the law and the prophets: 'He loved the Scriptures, quoted from them constantly and never once intimated that they might be wrong.'"
> Billy went out in the forest and wandered up the mountain, praying as he walked, 'Lord, what shall I do? What shall be the direction of my life?' He had reached what he believed to be a crisis.

He saw that intellect alone could not resolve the question of authority. He must go beyond intellect. He thought of the faith he used constantly in daily life: he did not know how a train, or a plane or a car worked, but he rode them. He did not know why a brown cow could eat green grass and yield white milk, but he drank milk. Was it only in the things of the spirit that such faith was wrong?

Graham later described his own thoughts: "So I went back and I got my Bible and I went out in the moonlight. And I got to a stump and put the Bible on the stump, and I knelt down, and I said, 'Oh God: I cannot prove certain things, I cannot answer some of the questions Chuck Templeton is raising, some of the other people are raising, but I accept this book by faith as the Word of God.'"[2]

What had Graham done? In humble faith he had placed his doubts and questions into the hands of his Creator. He had humbled himself to admit that he did not have every answer, but that he could trust this God for the answers that he did not have. What followed, almost immediately, can only be attributed to the God who "revives the heart of the contrite." Two months later, Billy Graham launched his first Los Angeles evangelistic crusade. It was monumental beyond hope. So many thousands of people were converted and so many multitudes of Christians were revived that the crusade committee extended the campaign from three weeks to eight. The attendance was unheard of, as were the numbers of conversions. Many Hollywood personalities, as well as underworld characters were converted. Many gave instantaneous witness to the change in their lives.

The final service alone drew nine thousand people to an old revival tent. This was by far the largest evangelistic crusade in America in over thirty years!

Time and *Newsweek* both wrote about the "new" evangelist, Billy Graham. The Associated Press carried dispatches nationwide. Billy Graham's ministry suddenly accelerated around the world. He became a newsworthy figure. The work of God became something that the secular press would write about, a phenomenon that had not been true in America for decades.

And why had all this happened? In my opinion, it happened because one man, William Franklin Graham, Jr., was willing to humble himself before God, yield his own will, his possessions, his ministry, even his doubts, to the Lord of the universe and let Him make good on His promises to dwell with the humble and contrite of heart and to "revive the spirit of the lowly and revive the heart of the contrite."

Why couldn't such an impact be made on your campus? Why couldn't you and a small group of other believers prostrate yourselves, mentally, spiritually and emotionally, before the God of the universe, yielding up your rights, your possessions, your future and perhaps even your doubts. Then tell Him that though you are weak, He is strong, and while you are unable, He is able, able to produce a spiritual explosion on your campus that will set forth a movement that will last for decades.

How about you? Have you felt the need of God in this way? Has the need to humble yourself taken hold of you?

If not, why not take a few minutes right now and meditate on this passage, Isaiah 57:15, and its implications for you and your campus.

Why not tell God that you're willing to lay all before Him, your very life, your future, your studies, your money, your ministry and your doubts and fears. Ask Him to make good on His promise to revive you and your friends. Then begin to watch the miracles happen.

If you and your Christian friends will do this, then you are ready to enter into the third pre-requisite for revival and awakening.

5

Confession and Repentance

There is no awareness of sin. When you have a
revival, people are distressed by their sin; they
change and the culture changes.
                              James Montgomery Boice[1]

Perhaps you heard about the man who jumped
in his car, turned on the ignition, put the car in
drive, revved the accelerator, revved it again, but
could not get the car to move. He put his foot on
the gas again and again. The engine revved, the
transmission whined; but the car would not move.
What was the problem? The parking brake was
still engaged. No matter what he did, the man
could not get the car to move because the brake
was still on.

In our thinking so far, we have discussed first,
recognizing the need for revival, and second, humbling ourselves before God. These are the first two
prerequisites to our being involved in preparing
the way for a revival. And, now, to get the car
to go, to see a revival begin, indeed to get our-

selves revived, we have to take off the parking brake. This involves confession of and repentance from sin.

Sin is the great curse of life. It was the downfall of Adam and Eve. It meant the human race needed redemption from the pit into which it had put itself. Sin necessitated the Sin Bearer Himself, Jesus Christ, to take our sins on Himself in order that we might have fellowship with God.

Sin is the great non-conductor. It blocks the strong flow of God's power. It makes Christians fruitless and impotent. It causes them to bring shame to the name of Christ. The psalmist wrote, "If I regard iniquity in my heart, the Lord will not hear me" (Psalm 66:18).

There's no question about it. Revival and spiritual awakening on your campus are blocked by sin. This sin takes many different forms. Of course, there are the obvious, gross acts: drunkenness, drugs, immorality (that's right, sleeping with somebody before marriage *is* sin), cheating, etc.

In fact, the tragedy of our day is that many Christians participate in some or all of these and aren't even *aware* that they are committing sin. They are destroying themselves and are blocking any sort of fellowship with God.

For example, Proverbs 7:6-23 describes those who commit immorality. Verses 22 and 23 describe the final result of such sin. It is not pleasant: "Suddenly he follows her, as an ox goes to the slaughter... until an arrow pierces through his liver, as a bird hastens to the snare, so he does not know that it *will cost him* his life."

The seriousness of such sin cannot be overemphasized. Recently, at one university where I was lecturing on "Sex, Love and Marriage," a young Christian woman told me, "Dan, what you say makes sense. I am going to quit sleeping with my boyfriend. I never knew it was wrong. Now I know why I have been miserable."

You see, sin is fun for a season, but it is a short season. It brings physical, emotional, and spiritual devastation. The tragedy is that Christians get involved in these things more and more deeply and thereby reduce both their fellowship with God and the ultimate abundance of life that Christ has planned for them.

It is important to state at this point, however, that sin runs far more deeply than just the obvious outward acts. Romans, Chapter 3, verse 23, aptly states, "All have sinned and fall short of the glory of God." That "all" refers not only to those who appear to be blatantly sinful, but also to each of us who hide our disobedience.

Coldheartedness, lukewarmness, criticism, back-biting, prayerlessness, and caring more about the approval of others than the approval of God, are definitely sinful attitudes and actions.

Compromise with evil in order to make the grade, cheating, lying (even little white ones), unrestrained anger against a brother or sister in Christ, uncaring attitudes toward the lost, and general boredom with spiritual issues, all fit the category of subtle, often "acceptable" sins.

Such a list could go on and on, could it not? Racism, hatred, envy and conscience-troubling issues. They all qualify as sin. Therefore, we all qualify as sinners.

The issue at hand is not whether we *are* sinners, but what will we do about our sins?

Sin short-circuits God's mighty power. Before He can bring revival and spiritual awakening, we who are burdened for it and are humbling ourselves before Him must ourselves be cleansed and changed. When we are different, others can be drawn to be different also.

Every revival found in Scripture and in more modern history has included confession and repentance from sin.

J. Oswald Sanders shows this fact clearly in his report of the Hebrides' (Scottish) Revival:

> Around 1950, there was a powerful movement of the Spirit in the Hebrides. The awakening did not just happen. For some months a number of men met three nights a week for prayer; they often spent hours. The weeks passed and nothing happened until one morning at about two o'clock. A young man read Psalms 24, verses 3 to 5, "Who may stand in his holy place? He who has clean hands and a pure heart, who has not lifted up his soul to falsehood and has not sworn deceitfully. These shall receive a blessing from the Lord."
>
> He closed the Bible and looking at his companions on their knees before God, he cried: "Brethren, it is just so much humbug to be waiting thus night after night, month after month, if we ourselves are not right with God. I must ask myself, is my heart pure, are my hands clean", and at that moment something happened. God swept into that prayer group and at that wonderful moment seven (7) Elders discovered what they evidently had not discovered before, that revival must be related to Holiness... they found themselves in the searching power of the presence of God and discovered things about themselves they had

never suspected. That the blood of Calvary heals and cleanses… these men found themselves lifted to the realm of the supernatural. These men knew that revival had come.[2]

Let me be clear just what confession and repentance entail. One of the classic biblical texts on this issue is Proverbs 28:13: "He who conceals his transgressions will not prosper, but he who confesses and forsakes them will find compassion."

From this verse, it is obvious that we should not conceal our transgression. Concealing is called hypocrisy and will lead to disaster in our Christian lives. Be honest. Too often I have spoken to business and professional people who say, "Dan, I faked people out in high school and college. I put on a Christian front, but inside I was a liar. Since I left college I have quit the Christian life altogether; I no longer want to be a hypocrite."

Honesty is the first step in confession and repentance. We must be genuine if we are to seek revival. Relax. God knows what we are really like. We don't have to pull the wool over anyone's eyes. Christ wants to be who He is in terms of who He is making us, not in terms of our building our "image."

Confession: To Agree With God

Confession is the next step. Basically, it means "to agree with God," to say the same thing as God. When we confess our sin it means two things. First, it means I call sin wrong and do not gloss over it or blame it on some other person or circumstance. I take responsibility for it and admit my error.

Second, I agree with God that Christ died for that sin and that it was forgiven at the cross. He died for all my sins, even the ones I commit ten years from now. I agree that He has paid the price and I accept by faith that fact for myself for that particular sin.

Confession involves exercising faith in the promises of God. First John 1:9 tells us that "if we confess our sins, He is faithful and righteous to forgive us our sins and to cleanse us from all unrighteousness." That is a promise. To make it true in our experience, we must trust it, rely upon it and have faith in it; then it becomes effective in our lives.

Confession means that I bring each individual sin before God. I acknowledge it as wrong and also thank Him that it is forgiven. I do not seek to hide it. Rather, I acknowledge it.

In 1970 at Asbury College in Wilmore, Kentucky, an awakening occurred that illustrates this need for confession.

It began when a few concerned students began to meet to pray for spiritual awakening. On February 3, Asbury students went to a normal 10 A.M. chapel service. As sometimes happened, the dean did not give a message but instead asked students to share testimonies.

Those who came forward were unusually fervent in telling what God was doing in their lives. One senior said "I am not believing that I am standing here telling you what God has done for me. I have wasted my time in college up to now, but Christ has met me, and I am different. Last night the Holy Spirit flooded in and filled my life and now for the first time ever, I am excited about being a Christian." As the end of the chapel hour approached, the bell sounded for classes to begin, but went unheeded.

Students confessed sins such as cheating, stealing, bitterness and drug use. The editor of the school newspaper had skipped chapel, but when he heard what was going on he came and hid in the corner. Eventually the Holy Spirit touched him: "I knew things in my life were a lie. . . . I was a sick and miserably lonely young man. Yet I sat there for two hours refusing to do anything. . . there came that critical moment when I was forced to admit that my self sufficiency was failing me and I needed to be dependent upon Jesus Christ. I prayed at the altar for an hour and a half undergoing a spiritual revitalization."[3]

Sometimes sins need to be confessed publicly like those of the editor above. Sometimes sins are confessed properly only to the Lord. J. Edwin Orr states that the rule of thumb in how much public confession should be made is "just enough to enlist the prayers of people right with God. The public confession of secret private sins might be dangerous."[4] Public sins should be confessed publicly, private sins confessed privately.

Repentance: To Change Your Thinking

We come now to the area of repentance. Repentance does not mean (as most people think) to feel sorry about your sin. Remember Proverbs 28:13 ". . . he who confesses and forsakes (his sin) will find compassion." Indeed godly *sorrow* for sin may *produce* repentance, but sorrow is not itself repentance. Repentance, the Greek word *metanoia,* means to change your thinking. Implied is a change of action, of direction. It involves forsaking sin. No one who repents of his sin can go on consciously committing it without remorse.

We confess our sins, and then, as we depend upon the Holy Spirit's power, we turn from them. The Spirit is the author of our conviction. He is also the source of our power to change. As we believers confess our sins and repent of them very specifically, we experience God's forgiveness, His cleansing, and a fresh infusion of holiness from the Holy Spirit Himself.

Repentance always brings results that affect all that we do. Students quit drunkenness. Sexual immoralities cease. Members of the opposite sex treat each other with respect, not as objects to gratify their own urges. Cheating ends, theft stops, backbiting and unjust criticism become things of the past. In other words, in times of real confession and repentance, lives and situations dramatically change.

Restitution: Repayment

Sometimes, restitution needs to be made as well. Restitution means repayment. If I have sinned against someone by word or deed, I may need both to ask their forgiveness and to make some sort of repayment for what I have done. This is one of the hardest corollaries of confession and repentance. For example, if I have cheated on a test, I need to tell the professor. It may cost me a great deal. It may cost me my place in college, or it may cost me a grade in that course, but it will not cost me nearly as much as refusing to make restitution will. If I have stolen, I need to repay. If I have assassinated someone's character, I must make it right with that person.

Dr. Stephen Olford reports this illustration of the results of restitution.

> During a time of spiritual awakening in Africa, we are told that the police authorities were astounded at the genuine repentance and restitution that was made not only by converts, but by backsliders who were restored to the Lord. *The Daily Dispatch,* of East London, South Africa listed the following articles returned by repentant believers: 80 sheets, 25 blankets, 24 jackets, 34 trousers, 11 overcoats, 6 women's coats, 25 dresses, 27 skirts, 50 shirts, 22 bedspreads, 64 hats, 23 towels, 1 table, 4 chairs, 50 pillow slips, 15 scissors, 5 hairclippers, 9 wallets, 4 cameras, 4 wristwatches, 3 revolvers and ammunition, 30 tumblers and an assortment of jewelry, tools, cigarette lighters, crockery, cutlery, boots, shoes, pressure stoves, frying pans, lanterns, and safety razors.[5]

One of my most vivid examples of restitution came last year. A Christian leader of my acquaintance made one small disparaging comment about another brother in Christ in a meeting that I attended.

Sometime later, the Lord convicted this leader of his sin of unwarranted criticism, and he confessed it to the Lord. Yet, he knew he must make restitution. He got on the phone and called all twelve of us who were in that meeting (most on long-distance calls) to confess to us his sin of criticism and to repent of his comments. He also phoned the individual about whom he had made the comment and confessed it. My respect for him soared. The calls cost him time, money, and effort; but the benefits far outweighed the costs.

In an earlier chapter we spoke of Evan Roberts, the collegian who, on the human level, inaugurated the Welsh Revival of 1905. Dr. Orr, the great chronicler of that event, described the effects of that awakening with its subsequent repentance by Christians upon Welsh society.

> The influence of the revival upon life in Wales was beyond calculation. Crime was so greatly diminished that magistrates in certain counties were presented with white gloves, signifying not a case to try. Drunkenness was cut in half, and a wave of bankruptcies swept the taverns of the principality. Profanity was curbed, until it was said that the *pit ponies* in the mines could not understand the orders.
>
> Throughout the revival and for many months afterwards all the churches of Wales were crowded with worshipers. Not only on Sundays but weeknights as well. Extraordinary conversions were reported and the most unusual instances of restitution of wrong. There was such an improvement in public morals that local authorities met to discuss what to do with the police forces, unemployed on account of the revival. All were agreed that the ethical transformation was tremendous.[6]

If our campuses are to see spiritual awakening, we Christians must be cleansed. We cannot hold on to sin, short-circuiting God's mighty power. When we confess our sin and repent of it, we are cleansed vessels, available for the Holy Spirit to use us and fill us. We are able to be powerful in our walk with Christ in our witness. Our prayers will start to be answered in greater abundance and fruitfulness.

If we will not confess and repent, the Holy Spirit is grieved and quenched. No fire of God will fall upon our campus—at least none resulting from our efforts.

You who are burdened for your campus, for the work of God to fill your college or university, will you not agree before God now to confess the sins He lays on your heart, repent of them, make restitution when necessary, and be available to be filled with God's mighty power by faith?

Here is an exercise that has worked well for thousands of students. Take a sheet of paper, a pencil, and your Bible. Ask the Holy Spirit to show you any areas that are displeasing Him. Take thirty minutes to an hour to make a list of those sins.

Then, tell the Lord you acknowledge them as sin and also accept by faith (1 John 1:9) His forgiveness. Determine by His power to turn from them and expect the Holy Spirit to fill you with His power. Make restitution or public confession where necessary. It may be tough; but believe me, it will be worth it. Once you have done this, if you were sincere, you are a cleansed vessel ready to become a glowing spark of revival and awakening on your campus. You are ready to be involved in the fourth prerequisite of spiritual awakening: praying fervently that such a revival will come. We will cover this in the next two chapters.

6

The Supreme Example of Prayer

The great people of the earth today are the people who pray. I do not mean those who talk about
prayer; nor those who say they believe in prayer;
but I mean those people who take time and pray.
These are the people today who are doing the
most for God; in winning souls; in solving problems; in awakening churches; in keeping the old
earth sweet awhile longer.

S. D. Gordon[1]

Arthur Wallis has answered so well the question
for us, "If Christ and the Father are always at
work in the world (John 5:17), why do we need
some special work, a revival, anyway?"

"There was once an ancient reservoir in the hills
that supplied a village community with water. It
was fed by a mountain stream and the overflow
from the reservoir continued down the streambed
to the valley below. There is nothing remarkable
about this stream. It flowed on its quiet way without even disturbing the boulders that lay in its
path or the foot bridges that crossed it at various
points. It seldom overflowed its steep bank or
gave the villagers any trouble. One day however,

some large cracks appeared in one of the walls of the old reservoir and soon afterwards the wall collapsed and the waters burst forth down the hillside. They rooted up great trees; they carried along boulders like playthings; they destroyed houses and bridges and all that lay in their path. The streambed could not now contain the volume of water which therefore flowed over the countryside, even inundating distant dwellings. What had before been ignored or taken for granted, now became an object of awe and wonder and fear. From far and near, people who in the usual way never went near the stream hastened to see this great sight."[2]

In the same way, like the gentle stream, God is always at work. But when He comes in exceptional and sweeping power, like a raging torrent, this is revival. Nothing is ever the same. People who have never thought about God now think of no one else, talk of no one else, and concentrate on no one else.

God desires to come in power to our campuses. He wants to come like this raging torrent to overturn the things that stand in His way on the campuses of America today. We as Christians have a fantastic opportunity to be used to prepare the way for such a movement.

Confession of and repentance of our sins, including any needed restitution, is vital to preparing us for laying hold of God and beseeching Him to move in all of His fullness in revival power. Having discussed previously the importance of *recognizing* the need for spiritual awakening, *humbling* ourselves before God, and *confession and repentance,* we now come to the fourth prerequisite for preparing the way for a mighty torrent of God's grace and power. Namely, the need to pray fervently, persistently, and consistently for spiritual awakening on our campuses.

Prayer for revival, not for Aunt Sally's sciatica or Cousin Herman's toothache, but for genuine spiritual awakening, is the channel through which God's revival power flows. We must pour out our hearts for the salvation of our family and friends, for our campus, for the morals of our country, in a fresh way. This stimulates our faith and demonstrates to God that we are serious about our requests. He then answers those prayers by coming and bringing a fresh spiritual awakening.

Never in history has there appeared any vast spiritual movement without preceding, fervent prayer by a motivated group of believers. In fact, if you count the last two thousand years of Christianity as just such a movement, we find that it too was preceded immediately by three-and-one-half years of fervent prayer effort by one individual, Jesus Christ.

In fact, it was my own study into His personal prayer life that made radical changes in my habits of prayer and has added new power to my life and ministry. It was also this study that launched my *burden* for awakening, which I hope you are starting to share. In this chapter we shall examine several aspects of Christ's sublime prayer life, which I hope will be a motivation to us to move forward in our own prayers. Perhaps the end of such a study will be that we may be used to see God work mighty miracles on our own campuses for His glory.

Although Jesus was fully God, He was also fully human. He, as a man, depended upon God the

Father to meet His every need and to accomplish His entire ministry. There is a great deal of evidence in scripture that His prayers were the very channel through which God's power flowed into Him and enabled Him to do such mighty exploits.

For example, in Luke, Chapter 11, we see the disciples, after one year of following Him and observing His ministry. At this point, they were desiring similar results in their own lives and personal ministries, and they were about to ask Him to teach them how their ministries and lives could take on much of the same flavor.

The interesting element in Luke 11 is that when they asked Him to teach them they did not ask about the mechanics of His miracles. Rather, they came to Him with the question, "Lord, teach us to pray."

It is my conviction that these twelve men had begun to realize that the secret of the power and ministry of Jesus' life was the intimate prayer time he spent with His Father. They also realized that the only way that they themselves were going to experience a similar result was to learn how to tap into God through prayer in the same way.

Jesus was a master teacher of prayer, not just through His words but more so through His life. As we do a brief survey of His ministry, we shall see the tremendous importance of prayer in everything He said and did. I am hoping that this will motivate us to lay hold of God in the same way so that our lives and ministries can take on these same characteristics.

Beginning in Prayer

Let us look first at the way He began His ministry. In Luke 3:21, we read the words: "Now it came about when all the people were baptized, that Jesus was also baptized, and while He was praying, heaven was opened."

It is significant to note that at the very outset of Jesus' ministry He was praying. Indeed, it was while He was praying that heaven itself was opened and, we read later, that the Holy Spirit descended upon Him and God the Father spoke audibly. Jesus knew that before the launching of any great enterprise it was vital to spend time with the Father, talking to Him about the events that would subsequently occur and asking Him for His power to accomplish the task that was set before Him.

As I mentioned before, no great enterprise has ever been launched for God successfully without fervent prayer prior to it. The founding of Campus Crusade for Christ is such an example. Prior to 1951, Bill and Vonette Bright, the founders of Campus Crusade had done some evangelistic work at the UCLA campus with no memorable results. Then, in 1951, a 24-hour prayer chain for UCLA was started in the churches of Los Angeles. The day was divided into ninety six 15-minute periods with people praying around the clock for that campus.

Following the inauguration of this prayer movement, in the very first evangelistic meeting at a sorority house, over half the women present indicated they wanted to know Jesus Christ personally. In evangelistic meetings that followed with various fraternities, sororities and athletic teams, similar responses occurred, and hundreds of students found salvation in Jesus Christ.

In fact, by the end of that first year at UCLA, over 250 students were newly converted, including the most outstanding student leaders on the campus. As an added gift the campus chimes, which had previously played secular songs, now began to play hymns at noontime.

Continuing in Prayer

Not only did Jesus Christ begin His ministry in prayer, but He also continued in prayer throughout His earthly life. A verse that has galvanized me is Luke 5:16, which reads, "But He Himself would *often* slip away to the wilderness and pray." This verse refers to the *habit* of praying in Jesus Christ's life. The thing that was such a burr under my saddle was that He did it frequently. Prayer was not a haphazard emergency activity of our Lord. He was engaged in prayer as the norm of His life. One might ask, "Well, just when did He pray anyway? In what situations was prayer called for?" Oswald Sanders in his book, *Prayer Power Unlimited*, gives us a brief overview:

> He prayed in the morning at the gateway of the day (Mark 1:35). He prayed in the evening when the day's work was over (Mark 6:46).
>
> Great crises were preceded by prayer. It was while he was praying at His baptism that heaven was opened. This was the watershed of His life and ministry, for He was identifying Himself with the Godly remnant of the apostate nation.
>
> He prayed in the hour of His popularity, the

time when so many are swept off their feet.

His selection of the twelve apostles, a seemingly unimportant yet in reality epic making event in world history, was made only after a night of prayer (Luke 6:12-13).

It was after a special time of prayer that he opened His heart to his disciples and shared with them the dread fact of his approaching suffering and death (Luke 19:9-28).

It was while he was in the act of prayer that the majestic transfiguration scene was enacted and the approving and authenticating voice of His Father was heard (Luke 9:29, 35). Prayer was the cause, transfiguration was the effect. Is there a lesson here for us?

Great achievements were preceded by prayer. Many miracles followed prayer: the feeding of the four thousand, the feeding of the five thousand, walking on water, the raising of Lazarus, and the healing of the insane boy. Each of these miracles was linked with the prayer that preceded it.

Great achievements were followed by prayer. When confronted with great crisis, we turn instinctively to prayer, but once the crisis is over, the task achieved, we tend to lean on our own abilities or wisdom. Jesus guarded against this evil by following such occasions with prayer.

Great pressure of work was a call to prayer. Our Lord's life was exceptionally busy. He worked under constant pressure. At times He had no leisure even for meals. But whatever the pressure, He made sure that prayer did not become a casualty. To Him, it was a call to devote extra time to prayer.[3]

In short, Jesus prayed all the time. There was never a time when He did not pray to meet the tasks, the pressures, the burdens, and the joys of His day, of His week, of His year. One might get the impression that prayer was the consuming passion of His life.

Ending in Prayer

Not only did He begin in prayer and continue in prayer, but He also ended His ministry in prayer. On the night of His betrayal and capture He fortified Himself, as Luke 22 informs us, by going to the Garden of Gethsemane to fall on His knees and spend an extended time of prayer with His Father. He warned the disciples, "Pray that you may not enter into temptation." He Himself knew the reality of those words, that prayer was the antidote to temptation and sin. He knew that His temptation to do His own will could be counteracted by extended time with the Father. Where you and I might have found ourselves anxious and afraid and self-centered prior to bearing the sins of the whole world and suffering the cruel death of the cross, Jesus had eyes only for His Father and for His continued need to depend upon Him even at the end of His ministry.

But this is not the whole story of the end of His ministry. In fact, Luke 23:46 tells us that even His final words on the cross were a prayer to His Father: "And Jesus, crying out with a loud voice, said, 'Father, into Thy hands I commit my spirit.' Having said this He breathed His last."

One might ask, how could He end His life in such a prayerful way? The answer is that He could not have ended His life in such a way had it not been the habit of His life previously. Because the norm of Jesus' life was prayer, it was also the logical and most blessed way to end His life.

Praying Today

Yet, there is more. Jesus began in prayer, continued in prayer, and ended His ministry in prayer. But what is Jesus Christ doing today? There is a remarkable verse in Hebrews, chapter 7, verse 25, that tells us in what ministry Jesus engages now. "Hence also He is able to save forever those who draw near to God through Him, since He *always* lives to make intercession for them."

Jesus Christ in heaven today is continually praying for us. He has not stopped yet. The habit of His life on earth is the habit of His life in heaven. Indeed we are always on His mind, and He is always presenting us before the Father in His prayers.

S. D. Gordon commented, "The Lord Jesus is still praying. Thirty years of living; thirty years of serving; one tremendous act of dying; nineteen hundred years of prayer. What an emphasis on prayer!"[4]

He began in prayer, continued in prayer, ended His ministry in prayer, and He continues in prayer today. What an example to us of the importance of prayer!

If we are to see awakening on our campuses that will sweep our universities and change them for good and for God, we must learn to follow the example of our Savior and become men and women of prayer. Let me suggest that you begin to set aside at least fifteen minutes a day for personal prayer, to talk to God about the needs on your campus. It may be difficult in the beginning to find things to pray about for fifteen minutes, but as you persevere you will soon find that fifteen minutes is not enough.

In the next chapter, we will look more specifically at the way that you and I, through our prayers, can help bring revival and awakening to our campuses.

7

The Power of Fervent Prayer

What we are feeling for, imagining, longing for, *really praying for* is a worldwide awakening in the power of the Holy Spirit. This alone would be enough to meet our needs, to use our resources, and to incorporate our little personal stories of faith in a movement greater than anything the world has ever seen.

Sam Shoemaker[1]

Jesus is our example in prayer; we look to Him. Yet, we are also encouraged and challenged as we see how this fourth revival prerequisite of fervent prayer has been and is being applied to the task of bringing spiritual awakening to our world, especially to the campuses.

Prayer has always been the precursor to revival. If we will commit ourselves to such prayer, there is no limit to what we can see God do. Genesis 32:26 describes Jacob's struggle of with the angel of the Lord. Jacob's words are instructive: "I will not let thee go, except thou bless me" (KJV). That's the sort of fervency that needs to characterize our prayers. Pray for spiritual brushfire to break forth on our campuses to convert the lost, quicken the Christians, and focus the campus on Jesus Christ Himself. One may ask, "What can only a few of us praying, no matter how fervently, accomplish on a campus as large as ours?"

This chapter will give some examples that we can take to heart.

The Prayer of One Person

First, consider the example of one man, Elijah. James 5:17 tells us, "Elijah was a man with a nature like ours, and he prayed earnestly that it might not rain; and it did not rain on the earth for three years and six months."

He was a sinful, weak man, but he loved his great, powerful God. So, he prayed that it would not rain—not so his picnic would remain intact— but so that wicked King Ahab would be brought to his knees before the sovereign God of the universe.

God heard Elijah's prayer and He answered specifically. For three- and-a-half years there was no rain, not a drop. Famine and drought controlled the land. Finally Ahab was defeated.

Guess what Elijah did then. He prayed again. This time, he prayed it would begin to rain. And it poured. James' comment on all of this? "The effective prayer of a righteous man can accomplish much" (James 5:16).

Do you believe this? Then why not get on with that prayer for revival on campus? If you learn to be fervent in it, it will accomplish much!

Consider two other illustrations of what one

person's praying may accomplish. I quote from Charles Finney's *Revival Lectures:*

"In a certain town there had been no revival for many years; the church was nearly extinct. The youth were all unconverted, and desolation reigned unbroken. There lived in a retired part of the town an aged man of so stammering a tongue that it was painful to hear him speak. On one Friday, as he was at work in his shop, alone, his mind became greatly exercised about the state of the church and of the impenitent.

His agony became so great that he was induced to lay by his work, lock the shop door and spend the afternoon in prayer.

He prevailed and on the Sabbath called on the minister and desired him to appoint a conference meeting. After some hesitation the minister consented; observing however that he feared that few would attend. When evening came, more assembled than could be accommodated in the house. All were silent for a time, until one sinner broke out in tears, and said, if anyone could pray, kindly would he pray for *him?* Another followed, and another, and so on, until it was found that persons from every quarter of the town were under deep conviction. And what was remarkable was, that they all dated their conviction at the hour that the old man was praying in his shop. A powerful revival followed. Thus this old stammering man prevailed and as a prince had power with God.[2]

You see we are not talking about "spiritual giants" here. We are talking about ordinary people with a giant God who make an extraordinary effort to pray for an awakening.

Jesus said, "Again I say unto you, that if two of you shall agree on earth as touching anything that they shall ask, it shall be done for them of my Father which is in heaven" (Matthew 18:19 KJV).

Multiplying the Prayers of a Few

If one person praying for revival is good, two or more is better. Jonathan Edwards, one of the human channels of the First Great Awakening in America, said, "When God has something very great to accomplish for His church, it is His will that there should precede it, the extraordinary prayers of His people."

Consider a prayer meeting of a few college and post-college men in Philadelphia in 1857 and 1858. They became burdened for revival and launched a daily prayer meeting on November 23, 1857. At first, only a few attended, but they were not discouraged. They continued. Soon the room contained twenty, thirty, forty, sixty. The fervency of prayer increased. One could sense an explosion about to occur.

In March (four months after they began to pray) the revival began. J. Edwin Orr describes it for us.

> At first, only the small room was occupied, with a few in attendance. Then it became overflowing, and the meeting moved to the main saloon, meetings starting there on the tenth of March. Twenty-five hundred seats were provided, and were filled to overflowing. The sponsors next removed a partition from the main floor space and platform; next, the floor platform and lower gallery, then floor platform and both galleries filled up; fully six thousand people gathered daily.
>
> For months on end each separate church was opened at least each evening. Some of them as

often as three and five times a day and all were filled. Simple prayer, confession, exhortation and singing was all that happened, but it was so honest, so solemn, the silence so awful, the singing so overpowering, the meetings were unforgettable.

In order to continue the work, which flooded churches with inquirers and converts, a big canvas tent was bought for $2,000 and opened for religious services on May 1, 1858. During the following four months, an aggregate of 150,000 attended the ministry under the canvas, many conversions resulting. The churches in Philadelphia reported 5,000 converts thus won.[3]

These numbers are all the more amazing when you consider that the total population of Philadelphia at this time was less than a tenth of its current size. The nearby state of New Jersey, affected by the same revival and awakening, recorded over sixty thousand converts within a few weeks! During the same revival 40 percent of the students at Princeton were converted and 18 percent entered full-time Christian ministry.

Amazing! These were unknown individuals, not necessarily movers and shakers, not primarily fast trackers. Just ordinary folks. Yet through their prayers they were responsible for tens of thousands of converts and many more believers who became godly people. These percentages and numbers may seem mind-boggling in light of the spiritual apathy we often note among many of our classmates, but if we take our minds off of the numbers and place them on the pray-ers and their fervency in prayer for revival, we see that the same events can happen right now in our situations.

These people at whom we have looked had caught the "prayer spirit" of their Master. We can be infected in the same way today. Indeed, I believe that infection has already begun across our country and around the world.

Praying for Revival Today

Nearly weekly now I receive letters from students all over the country detailing their burden for prayer and revival. The great thing is that they have been putting their concern into action. Early in the morning, late at night, at noontime, students on hundreds of campuses are praying daily for revival at their schools.

Consider these tidbits:

In Kansas a professor reports praying daily for his fellow faculty members.

At one southern school students meet every Saturday morning at 6 A.M.(!) on the steps of their administration building to pray.

At Penn State, several years ago, thirty students banded together to pray for four fellows to be able to penetrate a country tightly closed to the gospel. The four succeeded.

Several major student movements have initiated plans to create by 1990 a nationwide network of one hundred thousand to pray daily for evangelization and discipling of every country in the world in this generation. Several months ago, David Bryant wrote these prophetic words: "For over two years, I have trained and coordinated cooperative prayer movements... ON EVERY HAND I HAVE BEEN CONFRONTED WITH AN INTEREST IN PRAYER—EVEN A

SENSE OF DIVINE TIMELINESS FOR IT—
TELLS ME THE HOUR IS RIGHT FOR A
SWEEPING PRAYER MOVEMENT...
NOTHING ELSE SEEMS *QUITE AS CRITICAL*
RIGHT NOW."

Time magazine's May 3, 1982, issue reports that
the most dramatic Christian revival in the world
today is in the country of Korea. The church is
growing at a rate of 6.6 percent per year, mostly
through conversions. It is projected that by the
year 2000, 42 percent of Korea will be Christian.
This is all the more amazing because in 1971 only
10 percent of Korea was considered Christian.

Think of it, the Christian population of a thirty
million person Buddhist country will have grown
from three million to twelve million in twenty nine
years!

How has it happened? There are many factors,
but consider the possible genesis of this movement
reaching back decades. J. Oswald Sanders tells
the story:

> Some years ago a great revival swept over Korea,
> the fruits of which revival remain to the present
> day. This revival had been prayed down. Four
> missionaries of different denominations had
> agreed to meet together to pray daily at noon. At
> the end of one month a brother proposed that "as
> nothing had happened," the prayer meeting
> should be discontinued. "Let us each pray at home
> as we find it convenient," said he. The others
> however protested that they ought rather to
> spend more time in prayer each day, so they con-
> tinued their daily prayer meetings for four
> months. Then suddenly the blessing began to be
> poured out.
>
> In less than two months more than two thou-

sand heathen were converted. In one church it was announced that a daily prayer meeting would be held every morning at four-thirty. The very first day four hundred people arrived long before the stated hour, eager to pray. The number rapidly increased to six hundred. Heathen people came to see what was happening. They exclaimed in astonishment, "The living God is among you!"[5]

Commenting on the above, Dr. Joon Gon Kim, respected Korean pastor and Campus Crusade for Christ East Asian Director, says:

In 1907 at Pyongyang seven hundred people were dramatically filled with the Holy Spirit while attending a weeklong Bible study conference. This conference is often referred to as the Korean Pentecost. The lives of those attending were changed. They began their new lives as fireseeds of prayer, founding a nationwide prayer movement *which continues today*. The fireseeds became witnesses for Christ, used mightily to start spiritual fires across our nation and into many corners of the world. Fireseeds traveled to China, Japan, and America. Anywhere Korean people assembled a spark seemed to ignite.[6]

You see, the Korean revival began in prayer, it continued in prayer, and it goes on now at an accelerated pace in prayer. Tomorrow morning at 4 A.M. and every morning at 4 A.M. millions of Koreans will rise, dress and go to homes and churches to pray for revival and the Christianization of their country.

Oh, if we in America will only catch their enthusiasm for prayer, what would we see here? Let me suggest that you do three things. First, begin to make a list of all the biblical promises on prayer, especially those relating to revival.

90

Second Chronicles 7:14 would be a good place to start.

Second, pray daily yourself for revival on your campus, in your dorm or Greek house. Ask God for greater fervency.

Third, join with others (or call them together yourself), who are praying for revival; two are better than one. Finally, I am including a quote that has for years pricked my own prayer life; I hope it will be equally stimulating to you. It is from Leonard Ravenhill.

> The church has many organizers, but few agonizers; many who pay, but few who pray; many resters, but few wrestlers; many who are enterprising, but few who are interceding. People who are not praying are playing.
>
> Two prerequisites of dynamic Christian living are vision and passion, both of these are generated by prayer. The ministry of preaching is open to a few. The ministry of praying is open to every child of God.
>
> The secret of praying is praying in secret. A worldly Christian will stop praying; a praying Christian will stop worldliness...
>
> Tithes may build the church, but tears will give it life. That is the difference between the modern church and the early church. Our emphasis is on paying, theirs was on praying. When we have paid, the place is taken. When they had prayed, the place was shaken (Acts 4:31).
>
> "In the matter of effective praying, never have so many left so much to so few. Brethren, let us pray.[7]

8

Calling Others to Pray

I am certainly not one of those who need to be
prodded. In fact, if anything, I am a prod.
Winston Churchill[1]

We have looked at four of the five human prerequisites to awakening thus far: recognizing the
need; humbling oneself before God; true confession and repentance; and fervent prayer for
revival by a small group. Now, we look at the fifth
and final link in this chain. It is this. *We must call
others to join with us in our passionate prayers.*

Winston Churchill, quoted above, said he was
a prod. Indeed, so it must be with us. Prodding
others to pray is the job of those of us who are
enthusiastic for it already. Everybody needs a
good swift kick in the area of prayer, and we are
the ones to provide it.

Revivals seem to work this way. A few people
are themselves revived. They begin to pray, and
pray, and pray for an awakening on campus, or
in their church, or their city. The more they pray,
the greater the burden becomes. They cannot

bear it alone anymore. They need others "under the rock" with them.

So they call others to blend their own hearts and prayers with the original few. God touches these new participants and they too are set on fire. They then recruit others as well. Thus, the numbers who are praying fervently increase.

Sooner or later, a "critical mass" of praying fervent believers is gathered. As in a nuclear reaction, when molecules of radioactive material are continuously added until a certain mass is reached, and an explosion occurs, so too, when a certain number (known only to God) of fervent praying believers who are laying hold of God for revival is reached, spiritual explosion occurs. God sends a sweeping movement to touch the campus, home, church and city, in order to revive believers and to awaken unbelievers so that they may be converted.

Such a gathering of like-minded souls follows the biblical principle of multiplication expounded many times in the Scriptures and exemplified in these two passages: "How could one chase a thousand and two put ten thousand to flight unless their Rock had sold them, and the Lord had given them up?" (Deuteronomy 32:30)

"And the things which you have heard from me in the presence of many witnesses, these entrust to faithful men who will be able to teach others also" (2 Timothy 2:2).

Both of these verses indicate that with greater numbers of committed believers more can be accomplished. If I infuse others with my burden for prayer and for awakening, they will in turn ignite additional people as well.

The Seed and the Fire

Dr. Joon Gon Kim of Korea calls such people "fireseeds," people who bear the *seed* of the gospel and the *fire* of the Holy Spirit. They become sparks of revival to set entire nations ablaze wherever they go.

Dr. Kim writes about these fireseeds and what he believes they can accomplish: "Fireseeds have no limitations. They can glow and grow and burn and blossom wherever they are planted.

"A fireseed cannot help but grow and multiply if he is equipped with the gospel and the power of the Holy Spirit. It only takes a fireseed to ignite spiritual fires which in turn set the world aflame."[2]

You may ask, "Has such a fireseed idea worked?" Consider Dr. Kim's results in Korea and around the world over the last fifteen years.

The fireseeds in Korea continue to spread in unusual ways. There are fireseeds in the Korean Navy. Presently 100 percent of the Navy ships have Bible study groups. Each begun by one of our fireseeds. Almost without exception every post of the Army has a Spirit-filled man in charge of leading a small group Bible study.

In the Hyundai Company of Illsan City, 327 Bible studies exist among twenty-one thousand workers. In schools, villages and among professionals we have fireseeds who are responsible to ignite spiritual flames.

A few days ago one very influential man who became a Christian through our ministry reported to me that in the Marine College where he holds a position, there are 120 ships, each with a small Bible study group of its own. The ships he ministers on range from small 500-ton ships to 30,000 ton commercial vessels.

One of our graduate students works for a stock company. This man is the original fireseed for 97 groups from between 5 and 40 people throughout his company. I met his 97 Bible study leaders and found them to be rapidly spreading fireseeds.

Fireseeds are also spreading overseas. In the Middle East countries our disciples are very active among the 150,000 Koreans employed there. In Thailand, the Philippines, and many other Asian countries our disciples are at work. Our fireseed disciples are involved in almost every Korean church in the United States.

We cannot trace how deep or wide our fireseeds are now aglow. But they will continue. By 1986 we are planning to establish 100,000 small groups across Korea. By 1990 there will be 1,000,000 groups led by 1,000,000 fireseed leaders.[3]

The Fellowship of the Burning Heart

Lest you think that such a gathering of like-minded souls to pray is simply an Asian phenomenon, let me set that notion at rest. This is a pattern which God is using all over the world. In the U.S., an example of a few revived people calling many to join them occurred in 1949 in California. Dr. Henrietta Mears of Hollywood Presbyterian Church had been conducting a collegiate conference at Forest Home, California. Several committed men joined her one night for prayer. In the midst of that prayer meeting, God touched all of them in a unique way that produced spiritual awakening in all who were there. During that prayer meeting, one discouraged pastor entered late, intending to tell Dr. Mears that he was leaving the ministry. Upon joining the group he,

96

too, was touched by God and found fresh meaning, purpose and power in his life from this small revival. Because they had been touched by God they wanted to call others to join them in prayer. They formed what they called the "Fellowship of the Burning Heart," which was committed to calling others to join them in prayer and work for spiritual awakening in our world. Amazing indeed are the results.

After that awakening, Dr. Bill Bright founded Campus Crusade for Christ. Today its staff numbers sixteen thousand in 151 countries around the world. Millions have found Christ through this movement.

Dr. Louis Evans, Jr. later became pastor of the National Presbyterian Church in Washington, D.C., where he now ministers to thousands weekly.

The discouraged pastor, Richard Halverson, stayed in the ministry, pastoring the Fourth Presbyterian Church, which is also in Washington. Today, he is Chaplain of the U.S. Senate, ministering to many who hold high office in our land.

Kenneth Scott Latourette, the dean of church historians, has informed us, "Our reading of Christian history has accustomed us to see God break forth in unexpected places where souls have opened themselves to Him and have been made great by the touch of His Spirit."[4] Calling others to pray for spiritual awakening is one way we can "be made great."

The Momentum Increases

David Bryant of Inter-Varsity Christian Fellowship has spearheaded a program called "Concerts of Prayer." Basically these are regular meetings to link campus, church, and mission agencies in prayer for awakening. Started only recently, the momentum is increasing for such prayer all over America.

On one campus, Clemson University, two students were burdened to pray every day at dinner for awakening on campus. They began to gather others. By the end of one nine-month term, over two hundred students were praying in that meeting, and the campus had been greatly affected. Scores of missionaries, pastors, and godly lay people came from that movement at Clemson and are serving Christ fruitfully around the world today.

A student I knew at Georgia Tech began to pray that God would touch the fraternity system on his campus for Christ. As far as I know, at that time he was the only one who was praying, and he really did not know how God would do it. As he prayed, he became more burdened and began to enlist some of his own Christian fraternity brothers, as well as those he had introduced to Christ, to pray with him and to work for the evangelization of the fraternity system on his campus. From that prayer group grew a Bible study in his house which eventually increased to as many as seventy men in that one fraternity. Other Christians began to hear about this movement and expressed a desire to pray and work for the evangelization of their own fraternities. At the end of that one year, there were well over two hundred fraternity men involved in Bible studies and outreach because one man enlisted others to pray with him. That man is not famous according to the world's standards nor has he made the history books, but he is every bit as influential as the Bill Brights and the Richard Halversons, because he has been obedient to God to pray and to call others to join with him.

All over this country I believe there are students just like you who could allow God to use them first to pray and then to call others to join with them in prayer for awakening and revival on their campuses. If that happens, every university in our land could soon be aflame for Christ.

Many of us who are reading this book right now believe we need to open ourselves to Him to allow Him to bring revival through us, but that is not enough. We must call others to join with us to share our burden. The more who join us in prayer, the faster revival will come. As Jack Taylor has said, "Prayer gets us in the channel of revivability." The more people who "tune into" this channel, the greater the number of awakened people and the sooner the awakening we have been discussing will come.

Who is taking the initiative on your campus to call others to pray? How about you? You may not feel able, but God, as Latourette said, can make you great. Who knows, you may be Chaplain of the Senate in thirty years, or be accomplishing even greater things.

Why not call someone you know and get together today for prayer? Plan to do it regularly. Gather others and then get ready for results.

9

The Results of Spiritual Awakening on Campus

> The really effective agency of religion in the life of the college was the revival... which brought so many... into church and into the ministry. Most college presidents and college faculties of this era felt that they or God... had failed a collegiate generation, if once during its four years there did not occur arousing revival.
>
> —Frederick Rudolph[1]

Can you believe that at one time in America, college presidents thought they had failed if there was no revival in a given four-year collegiate term? What would that be like today?

Imagine the president of your college or university apologizing to the seniors at graduation because there had been no spiritual awakening on campus during their collegiate stay. Well, such a time might be coming again—if we'll meet the criteria for our part in an awakening like those described in the previous chapters. Let's review these criteria:

1. We must recognize the need for spiritual awakening (and commit ourselves to do something about it).
2. We must humble ourselves before our great God.
3. We must confess our sins, repent of them, and make restitution where possible.
4. We must begin to pray fervently for spiritual awakening.
5. We must call others to join us in this endeavor.

Remember, God brings awakening. We cannot program Him. But He has told us what our part is in preparing a way for such a movement of His Spirit. The sooner we get on with it, the better. In this chapter, we will examine the probable results of such a coming spiritual awakening on your campus. What will it produce when it comes? What should we expect?

There are many results from revivals of the past and there are many promises from the Bible. The outworking of revival will fall into four areas:

1. Holiness of life for believers.
2. Obedience to God and His Word.
3. Increased power from God.
4. A massive movement of God's Spirit in evangelism.

Let's look more closely at each of these.

First, holiness of life for believers. This result almost goes without saying. As Christians, through prayer, enter into the channel of revivability, their lives straighten up. When revival comes, it touches many other Christians who have not been burdened previously by the Spirit for personal change.

The Spirit forcefully touches upon their sin, convincing them in power of their need to confess and repent and make restitution. Christian students then desire to lay aside their old habits and unholy lifestyles and walk in fellowship with Christ, who loves them so.

The Asbury College revival of 1970 is a great example of this. As we previously discussed, student prayer led to awakening in chapel one morning. Students began to give testimony to the changes Christ had produced in their lives. Then other students began spontaneously to rise, confess their sins publicly, and ask for forgiveness. All classes were closed down and the chapel service continued unabated for 185 hours, nearly eight days. Christian students found themselves ceasing immorality, drugs, drunkenness, cheating, and swearing. They began serious Bible study, evangelism, and honest work and began loving their neighbors.

But there was more.

They began to take the message of this revival all over the country to other Christian schools. In all, nearly forty colleges were affected directly or indirectly. Even a national TV cameraman sent by a major network to cover such an unusual "religious" happening was touched. Hearing the confessions and testimonies and seeing the obviously newly changed lives of students, he put down his TV camera, walked to the altar of the college chapel, knelt down and gave his life to

Jesus Christ. If the secular campuses and the Christian colleges of America were to be awakened, I believe hundreds of such conversions would occur.

Nothing is perhaps so detrimental to Christ's cause than believers who live like the world. Tragically, many Christian students today participate in immorality, cheating, drunkenness and other sins because Christ is not Lord of their lives. Non-Christians write off Christ and His salvation because of this. Never have we needed holiness more, nor perhaps seen it less.

Other demonstrations of holiness that we should expect when awakening comes are: abortions decreasing on campus, virginity prior to marriage increasing, and *Playboy* and *Penthouse* subscriptions going way down. Wouldn't it be great if they went out of business? We could hope for voluntary closing of campus taverns, as their owners see the changed lives among the students. Voluntary honor codes would spring forth. Even the tone of the campus newspaper would change to reflect new lifestyles. The fraternity and sorority system would reflect increased moral values. Indeed, in one fraternity, so many brothers became Christians, Bibles were given at initiations.

The second major result of awakening on campus will be obedience to God and His Word. This is closely tied to holiness and means that believers are willing to obey what God says. Revival is by nature a new subjecting of ourselves to God. Remember that one of the first steps toward preparing for revival is humbling ourselves before Him. So it is when revival comes. Christians simply begin to do what He says and quit trying to avoid it.

This means that they begin to study, honor, and believe God's Word. It becomes their textbook, one that supercedes all other textbooks. Instead of trying to explain away God's promises and commands, people start applying faith and obedience to them.

This new willingness to do what God says will have great impact not only on personal lifestyles (a willingness to love your enemy, for example) but in two other areas: *outreach* and *social problems.*

We will cover outreach later, but it is worth saying here that there never is revival of believers, personal or corporate, that does not lead almost immediately to a missionary concern for both apathetic believers and unreached non-Christians. Remember, it was Samuel Mills of Williams College who laid the challenge on a small group of men to evangelize their world with the words, "We *can* do this if we *will.*" Notice he did *not* say, "We will do this if we can." Such determination to do God's will in outreach is a characteristic result of real revival.

In the area of obedience in dealing with social problems, revivals have clear, though sometimes delayed, results. As revived believers begin to study the Word of God afresh, they discover it contains many commands dealing with the poor, the hungry, the defenseless, the imprisoned, and otherwise needy people. Until a revival comes, believers often care only for their own needs and not those of others, particularly if the others are "invisible" to their own social class or group.

Upon being revived, however, Christians are caught up with a need to help in a godly way. Throughout history, hospitals, orphanages, and half-way houses have been established by revived believers. Dr. James Montgomery Boice says, "The best things that have ever happened in history have been as a result of that kind of movement, whether the Great Awakenings or the revivals of Wesley and Whitfield."[2]

We could expect on campus a new concern for the unborn infants and their rights while maintaining compassion for their parents. We could expect to see a declining suicide rate and Christians being concerned about counseling those who are so depressed that they want to take their lives. We should see a student movement against ungodliness in the faculty and administration and for a representation of the cause of Christ in academics. We would see clear thinking about international politics and war, with open forums for all relevant convictions to be expressed in a responsible and unintimidated manner.

We could expect ethics to again have a place in the university setting, with a call to morality, not simply legality, in the business, medical and professional schools. All of this has happened before and can happen again. The awakenings of the 1800s, for example, were the catalysts for both the abolition of slavery and the lessening of alcoholism in American life. In England, a revived member of Parliament, William Wilberforce, stopped the British slave trade practically singlehandedly.

College students are among the most idealistic groups in the world. Awakening would give eternal perspective to that idealism and perhaps thrust new solutions of old problems before the eyes of a watching world.

The third result of revival is increased power from God. The Holy Spirit is the One who brings revival to people and locations. He is the power source for all we do.

Early in this book, I mentioned the impact on me of 1 Corinthians 4:20: "For the kingdom of God does not consist in words, but in power." The previous two results, holiness and obedience, would be impossible without power from God Himself to do what He commands. Whatever God requires, God supplies. Since He requires obedience, then He provides the power needed.

The Rev. Jack Taylor has said, "Revival is simply the release of the life of Christ in us." Jesus promised the Spirit as the One who will, in fact, release that life in us (John 14:17). Thus, when spiritual awakening comes, believers are motivated to give their lives totally to Him and greater power is the result. Rev. A. J. Gordon, a godly pastor from Boston, underlined this truth to Robert Wilder, a leader of the Student Volunteer Movement, that great student mission movement that came out of the revival of the late 1800s. He told him, "God is ready to give you the power of His Spirit, as soon as you are ready to obey Him."[3] Shortly after that the Student Volunteer Movement was born with the watch word: *The evangelization of the world in this generation.* From this beginning, it is estimated that over twenty thousand college students sailed as foreign missionaries during the next forty years. This was the greatest student missionary movement in history. One can only shake one's head in awe and admit that great power had been released as a result of Wilder's and others' willingness to obey God.

We could expect on your campus to view increased power to see prayers answered, power to see fatigue defeated; power to study effectively and have a ministry at the same time; power to stick by convictions; power to lead others to Christ, power to disciple true converts, power to defeat all the many temptations of the world, the flesh and the devil. By way of personal testimony, I can only say that since revival has come to my life, power to do God's will has greatly increased.

The fourth result of revival is a great movement of God's Spirit in evangelism. I suppose it would be easy to write an entire book about this result alone. I mentioned earlier that revival never comes without producing this result, a sweeping movement of evangelism. Consider again the Welsh revival of 1905. In the space of three months, one hundred thousand were converted of which eighty thousand were still in the churches five years later. Let me say that again: one hundred thousand converted to Christ in three months. If it weren't so well documented, it would be hard to believe.

Similar things are happening today in Korea. Time Magazine reported that twelve million Koreans will be Christians by the year 2000.

That means nine million converts in less than thirty years. Put another way, that is almost one thousand converts in South Korea alone *every day* for thirty years. Incredible!

How about on campus? We have mentioned revivals in the 1700s, 1800s, and in 1905, when as many as three-fourths of the student bodies of various universities were converted on campuses like Yale, Princeton, Cornell, and others. But some of these things are starting to happen today, too. Here are some examples.

In one secular university in Alabama of several thousand students, nearly 10 percent of the student body is trained every week in evangelism and discipleship and every person on campus is being reached every year for Jesus Christ.

At the University of Miami in Oxford, Ohio, this past year, Christian students shared their faith with virtually every student on campus.

At one major university of twenty thousand students, the Christians are mapping plans to expose the entire campus to the gospel in a one-year period of time and to follow up all the new converts.

At a campus on the east coast, a sophomore said to me, "Dan, our objective here is to see 250 students so revived and so expectant that spiritual awakening will come to the entire campus."

When a revival comes, thrusts such as these become the norm, not the exception. This occurs not only because the believers are revived in their holiness, obedience and power, but also because the unbelievers are more deeply convicted of their sin and need for Christ. Such great numbers of unbelievers desire to come to Christ that believers are *forced* to tell them how to know Him. As Dr. Orr says, "In times of revival we believers must work like doctors in an epidemic." But what a glorious epidemic! I will be glad to pay that price, how about you?

When revival comes to your campus then, you may expect great zeal for reaching the lost on the part of Christians, unusual conversions occurring regularly, campus atheists receiving Christ, phone calls in the night from people asking how to be saved, enemies of the gospel brought into Christ's kingdom, evangelism and follow-up training classes numbering one thousand or more each week preparing believers to carry on the work, and Jesus Christ becoming the central issue of every segment of campus life.

Dr. J. Sidlow Baxter was asked by a friend of mine what it was like when revival came to his church in Edinburgh, Scotland, years ago. He replied, "I can only say that anywhere and everywhere you went God was in the atmosphere." God everywhere in the atmosphere. That's what you can expect on your campus. Wouldn't it be different from the atmosphere you experience there now?

Well, there is much more that might be said about the results of revival. We have touched on holiness, obedience, power and evangelism. Actually, God will probably surprise us all when He comes to your situation. He is the God of the unexpected and does far more than we could ever hope or ask or think. But one thing we can know for sure. When He does come, no one will be able to miss it. His movement is going to be powerful, it is going to be sweeping, and it's going to be significant for virtually every student, administrator and faculty member on your campus.

It seems to me that an appropriate action point for you would be to make an idea list of what you and your cohorts believe God could do on your campus when revival comes. Include names and places as God gives them to you. Your list might include things like: the dean of students becoming a witnessing Christian, or a particular dorm having five hundred or more in Bible studies every week, or a certain person's ceasing their drunkenness and immorality, etc., etc.

Dream big. Then begin to ask God to do the things you are putting on your list, and even to expand your vision to believe Him for greater things. As William Carey said, "Expect great things from God; attempt great things for God." Let's expect our campuses to explode in spiritual awakening soon.

10

Conclusions

It is my sincere prayer that the burden which
God has given me for spiritual awakening in our
day may be the heart-cry for revival of all who
read these pages. —Stephen F. Olford[1]

Some years ago Stephen Olford penned a book
called *Lord, Open the Heavens*. The above words
are found in his author's note at the beginning
of the book. I have included them because they
express exactly how I feel about the need for
awakening on the college campuses of America
today.

I believe with all my heart that revival on campus is not only needed, it is crucial. I also believe
that it is coming. If it does not come, I see very
little hope that the darkness which is beginning
to fall both intellectually, as well as morally and
ethically, on the colleges and universities of our
country will be lifted at any time prior to the
Lord's return. No doubt if there is no revival
many will still be won to Christ and many will be
discipled. But I do not see any way that the influence of unbelief of our day can be reduced,

apart from the sweeping movement of the Spirit of God.

As I mentioned, I think revival is coming. I think there is a tidal wave of dissatisfaction growing among Christian students today in the spiritual apathy that exists. I think there is a growing movement to pray for revival and to meet God's prerequisites for being fireseeds and channels of this revival on their campus. Examples from the distant past and more recent examples of revivals on campus, as well as current events, indicate to me that the Spirit of God is doing something highly significant, perhaps something that has not happened since 1905, the time of the last great student awakening in America.

The five steps toward preparing a way for revival that permeate this book are beginning to permeate the thinking of students around the country. By way of review, let me list them again.

First, God's people must recognize the need for revival.

Second, God's people must humble themselves before Him.

Third, God's people must confess their sins and repent of them, making restitution where necessary.

Fourth, God's people must begin to pray fervently and consistently for spiritual awakening.

Fifth, God's people must call others to pray as well.

The movement of people meeting these conditions is swelling. Frankly, I think all of us reading this book need to be a part of it and not miss what God is doing. Our tendency might be to become trapped in our own apathy, materialism and "the way we've done it for years" thinking. The time for business as usual is over, however. It is time for some new beginnings or, rather, it is time to be a part of the new beginnings that God is already bringing to pass.

By the time this book is published, twenty-five thousand or more college students and college-bound high school seniors will be gathered in Kansas City at a conference called KC '83 to learn how they can help bring spiritual awakening to their campuses. This represents nearly one out of every four hundred college students in the United States learning how to become spiritual fireseeds to go back to their campuses to help bring spiritual awakening. This event will be the largest single gathering of Christian college students in America's history. This conference bodes well in an exciting way for the future of revival on the campus.

Such a gathering is sorely needed. So often Christian students who want to see God work in an explosive way on their campuses are isolated and do not realize what God is doing in other places.

More seriously than that, it is important to understand that we are in a battle on the campus for the minds and souls of men and women. The stakes are not simply temporal but eternal. The destiny of the world is involved, not simply our own comfort. In fact, I believe that the greatest hope of our globe is revived university students, as yet unfettered by mortgages, mediocrity or man-made distractions, relentlessly serving Christ. Imagine men and women on their campuses calling the universities of our country to allow Jesus Christ back on the campus, to allow Him to be Lord of all.

If we fail to heed the rallying cry of our great Captain, Jesus Christ, to believe and pray for awakening, then the enemy of our souls will come in like a flood and we will find ourselves trapped by our own inaction and uncaring attitudes. Worse than that, we will have dragged hundreds of thousands of others down with us into the morass of our own indifference.

The purpose of this book is to ask you to commit yourself to become one of the fireseeds, one of the insurgents for spiritual awakening on your campus, praying and believing God to do something sweeping in your situation. If you do this, I believe your life will be significant beyond anything you could have ever hoped or asked or thought, in terms of making a difference not only in our country but in the lives of many countries around the world.

If you don't do it, then you will probably fall into the snare of mediocrity in which the average college student finds himself in college and beyond. You will probably end your life asking the question, "What did I accomplish of significant or eternal value? I wonder why I was ever here at all."

Commit yourself today to be one of these insurgents, a member of Christ's special forces who is praying and working and expecting the Lord to revive believers on campus and awaken unbelievers to the glory of His name.

In summary, consider this statement from a speech by Winston Churchill given during World War II. The occasion of the speech was Hitler's massing of forces on the coast of France for a probable invasion and attack upon Great Britain, the small island that lay between him and total European conquest. On the eve of this attack, Churchill made a speech that was used greatly in rallying all of England to stave off the coming disaster. His call in this speech, on a physical and wartime level, is the same call that I would like to leave with you on a spiritual level. See if you cannot hear in these words the voice of God speaking to you about your part in the revival to come.

"What General Weygand called the Battle of France is over. I expect that the Battle of Britain is about to begin. Upon this battle depends the survival of Christian civilization. Upon it depends our own British life and the long continuity of our institutions and our empire. The whole fury and might of the enemy must very soon be turned on us. Hitler knows that he will have to break us in this island or lose the war. If we can stand up to him, all Europe may be free and the life of the world may move forward into broad sunlit uplands. But if we fail, then the whole world, including the United States, including all that we have known and cared for, will sink into the abyss of a new dark age made more sinister, and perhaps more protracted, by the lights of perverted science. *Let us therefore brace ourselves to our duties, and so bear ourselves that, if the British Empire and its Commonwealth last for a thousand years, men will still say, "This was their finest hour.'* "[2]

May this be America's college and university students' "Finest Hour."

Notes

Chapter 1

1. Campus Crusade for Christ Staff, *How to Make A Mark That is Hard to Erase,* San Bernardino, CA: Campus Crusade for Christ, 1982, pp. 5-6.
2. Charles Finney, *Revival Lectures,* Westwood, NJ: Fleming H. Revell, p. 33.

Chapter 2

1. Clarence P. Shedd, *Two Centuries of Student Christian Movements,* New York: Association Press, 1934, p. 1.
2. Timothy C. Wallstrom, *The Creation of a Student Movement to Evangelize the World,* Pasadena, CA: William Carey International University Press, 1980, pp. 24,25.
3. J. Edwin Orr, *Campus Aflame,* Glendale, CA: Regal Books, 1971, p. 27.
4. Ibid, p. 101.

Chapter 3

1. Aleksander Solzhenitsyn, "A World Split Apart," *National Review,* July 7, 1978, p. 836.
2. Stephen Olford, *Lord, Open the Heavens,* Wheaton, IL: Harold Shaw, 1980, p. 92.

Chapter 4

1. John R. Mott, *Christian Students and World Problems,* New York: Student Volunteer Movement, 1924, p. 52.
2. John Pollock, *Billy Graham: The Authorized Biography,* Grand Rapids, MI: Zondervan Publishing House, 1966, p.52.

Chapter 5

1. "Interview with James M. Boice," *Discipleship Journal,* Issue 11, 1982, p. 43.
2. J. Oswald Sanders, *Prayer Power Unlimited,* Chicago: Moody Press, 1977, p. 147,148.
3. "Eight Days That Shook Asbury," *Worldwide Challenge,* March 1983, p. 19.
4. J. Edwin Orr, *Campus Aflame,* Glendale, CA: Regal Books, 1971, p. 231.
5. Stephen F. Olford, *Lord, Open the Heavens,* Wheaton, IL: Harold Shaw, p. 86.
6. J. Edwin Orr, *op.cit.,* p. 101,102.

Chapter 6

1. S. D. Gordon, *Quiet Talks on Prayer,* Westwood, NJ: Fleming H. Revell, 1967, p. 11.
2. Stephen F. Olford, *Lord, Open the Heavens,* Wheaton, IL: Harold Shaw, p. 62,63.
3. J. Oswald Sanders, *Prayer Power Unlimited,* Chicago: Moody Press, 1977, p. 28,29.
4. *Ibid.,* p. 33.

Chapter 7

1. Quoted in "Concerts of Prayer: Christians United in a Movement of Prayer for Spiritual Awakening and World Evangelization," David Bryant.
2. Charles Finney, *Revival Lectures,* Westwood, NJ: Fleming H. Revell, p. 72,73.
3. *Ibid.,* p. 137.
4. J. Edwin Orr, *Campus Aflame,* Glendale, CA: Regal Books, 1971, pp. 60,61.
5. J. Oswald Sanders, *Prayer Power Unlimited,* Chicago, IL: Moody Press, 1977, p. 154.
6. Dr. Joon Gon Kim, *Director's Letter, U.S. Campus Ministry,* "It Only Takes A Fireseed," Campus Crusade for Christ, April 27, 1982.
7. Leonard Ravenhill, "No Wonder God Wonders," Great Commission Prayer League.

Chapter 8

1. *Churchill, the Life Triumphant,* New York: American Heritage Publishing Co, Inc., 1965, p. 94.
2. Joon Gon Kim, "It Only Takes A Fireseed," *Director's Letter, U.S. Campus Ministry,* April 27, 1982, Campus Crusade for Christ.
3. *Ibid.*
4. J. Edwin Orr, *Campus Aflame,* Glendale, CA: Regal Books, 1971, p. 202.

Chapter 9

1. J. Edwin Orr, *Campus Aflame,* Glendale, CA, Regal Books, Glendale, CA 1971, p. 226.
2. "Interview with James M. Boice," *Discipleship Journal,* Issue 11, 1982, p. 43.
3. Timothy C. Wallstrom, *The Creation of a Student Movement to Evangelize the World,* Pasadena, CA: William Carey International University Press, 1980, p. 35.

Chapter 10

1. Stephen F. Olford, *Lord, Open the Heavens,* Wheaton, IL: Harold Shaw, 1980. p. 11.
2. *Churchill, The Life Triumphant,* New York: American Heritage Publishing Co., Inc., 1965, p. 91.